BRAIN GAMES™

Consultant: Elkhonon Goldberg, Ph.D.

Publications International, Ltd

Elkhonon Goldberg, Ph.D., ABPP/ABCN (consultant) is a clinical professor of neurology at New York University School of Medicine, a diplomate of the American Board of Professional Psychology/American Board of Clinical Neuropsychology, and director of The East-West Science and Education Foundation. Dr. Goldberg created the Manhattan-based Cognitive Enhancement Program, a fitness center for the brain, and is author of the internationally best-selling books *The Wisdom Paradox: How Your Mind Can Grow as Your Brain Grows Older* and *The Executive Brain: Frontal Lobes and the Civilized Mind*.

Contributing Writers: Elkhonon Goldberg, Ph.D., Holli Fort

Puzzlers: Cihan Altay, Clarity Media Ltd./www.clarity-media.co.uk, Myles Callum, Kelly Clark, Jeanette Dall, Mark Danna, Harvey Estes, Josie Faulkner, Connie Formby, Peter Grabarchuk, Serhiy Grabarchuk, Dick Hess, Marilynn Huret, David Millar, Alan Olschwang, Ellen F. Pill, Ph.D., Paul Seaburn, Fraser Simpson, Howard Tomlinson, Kirsten Tomlinson.

Additional Puzzle Editing: Jon Delfin

Illustrators: Connie Formby, Nicole H. Lee, Shavan R. Spears

Back Cover Puzzles: Myles Callum, Howard Tomlinson

ISBN-13: 978-1-4127-1451-8

ISBN-10: 1-4127-1451-6

Manufactured in China.

8 7 6 5 4 3 2 1

CONTENTS

BRAIN FITNESS

Your mind is your most important asset—more important than your house, your bank account, and your stock portfolio. You insure your house and work hard to pad your bank account. But what can you do to sharpen your mind and to protect it from decline? With the baby-boomer generation getting on in years, an increasing number of people are asking this question. Modern-day science provides a clear answer: Protect your mind by protecting your brain. To understand this relationship further, we turn to cutting-edge research.

Protect and Enhance Your Brainpower

Modern-day neuroscience has established that our brain is a far more plastic organ than was previously thought. In the past it was believed that an adult brain can lose only nerve cells (neurons) and cannot acquire new ones. Today we know that new neurons—and new connections between neurons—continue to develop throughout our lives, even well into advanced age. This process is called *neuroplasticity*. Thanks to recent scientific discoveries, we also know that we can harness the powers of neuroplasticity in protecting and even enhancing our minds at every stage of life—including our advanced years.

How can we harness neuroplasticity to help protect and enhance our mental powers? Recent scientific research demonstrates that the brain responds to mental stimulation much like muscles respond to physical exercise. In other words, you

have to give your brain a workout. The more vigorous and diverse your mental life—and the more you welcome mental challenges—the more you will stimulate the growth of new neurons and new connections between them. Furthermore, the *nature* of your mental activity influences *where* in the brain this growth takes place. The brain is a very complex organ with different parts in charge of different mental functions. Thus, different cognitive challenges exercise different components of the brain.

How do we know this? We've learned this by experiments created from real-life circumstances and *neuroimaging*, the high-resolution technologies that allow scientists to study brain structure and function with amazing precision. Some say that these technologies have done for our understanding of the brain what the invention of the telescope has done for our understanding of the planetary systems. Thanks to these technologies, particularly MRI (magnetic resonance imaging), we know that certain parts of the brain exhibit an increased size in those who use these parts of the brain more than most people. For example, researchers found that hippocampi, the parts of the brain critical for spatial memory, were larger than usual in London cab drivers who have to navigate and remember complex routes in a huge city. Studies revealed that the so-called Heschl's gyrus, a part of the temporal lobe of the brain involved in processing music, is larger in professional musicians than in musically untrained people. And the angular gyrus, the part of the brain involved in language, proved to be larger in bilingual individuals than in those who speak only one language.

What is particularly important is that the size of the effect—the extent to which the part of the brain was enlarged—was directly related to the *amount of time* each person spent in the activities that rely on the part of the brain in question.  For instance, the hippocampal size was directly related to the number of years the cab driver spent on the job, and the size of Heschl's gyrus was associated with the amount of time a musician devoted to practicing a musical instrument. This shows that cognitive activity directly influences the structures of the brain by stimulating the effects of neuroplasticity in these structures, since the enlargement of brain regions implies a greater than usual number of cells or connections between them. The impact of cognitive activity on the brain can be great enough to result in an actual increase in its size! Indeed, different parts of the brain benefit directly from certain activities, and the effect can be quite specific.

Diversify Your Mental Workout

It is also true that any more or less complex cognitive function—be it memory, attention, perception, decision making, or problem solving—relies on a whole network of brain regions rather than on a single region. Therefore, any relatively complex mental challenge will engage more than one part of the brain, yet no single mental activity will engage the whole brain.

This is why the diversity of your mental life is key to your overall brain health. The more vigorous and varied your cognitive challenges, the more efficiently and effectively they'll protect your mind from decline. To return to the workout analogy: Imagine a physical gym. No single exercise machine will make you physically fit. Instead, you need a balanced and diverse workout regime.

You have probably always assumed that crossword puzzles and sudoku are good for you, and they are. But your cognitive workout will benefit more from a greater variety of exercises, particularly if these exercises have been selected with some knowledge of how the brain works.

The puzzle selection for this second collection of *Brain Games*™ has been guided by these considerations—with knowledge of the brain and the roles played by its different parts in the overall orchestra of your mental life. We assembled as wide a range of puzzles as possible in order to offer the brain a full workout.

There is no single magic pill to protect or enhance your mind, but vigorous, regular, and diverse mental activity is the closest thing to it. Research indicates that people engaged in mental activities as a result of their education and vocation are less likely to develop dementia as they age. In fact, many of these people demonstrate impressive mental alertness well into their eighties and nineties.

What's more, the pill does not have to be bitter. You can engage in activities that are both good for your brain *and* fun.

Different kinds of puzzles engage different aspects of your mind and you can assemble them all into a cognitive workout regime. Variety is the name of the game—that's the whole idea! In any single cognitive workout session, have fun by mixing puzzles of different kinds. This book offers you enough puzzle variety to make this possible.

Welcome challenging puzzles, instead of feeling intimidated by them. Never give up! To be effective as a mental workout, the puzzles should not be too easy or too difficult. An overly easy puzzle will not stimulate your brain, just as a leisurely walk in the park is not an efficient way to condition your heart. You need mental exertion. On the other hand, an overly difficult puzzle will just frustrate and discourage you from moving forward. So it is important to find the "challenge zone" that is appropriate for you. This may vary from person to person and from puzzle to puzzle. Here, too, the gym analogy applies. Different people will benefit most from different exercise machines and from different levels of resistance and weights.

With this in mind, we have tried to offer a range of difficulty for every puzzle type. Try different puzzles to find the starting level appropriate for you. And before you know it, your puzzle-cracking ability will improve, your confidence will grow, and this will be a source of reassurance, satisfaction, and even pride.

Have Fun While Stretching Your Mind

It's important to have fun while doing something good for you. Puzzles can be both engaging and absorbing. An increasing number of people make regular physical exercise part of their daily routines and miss it when the circumstances prevent them from exercising. These habitual gym-goers know that strenuous effort is something to look forward to, not to avoid. Similarly, you will strengthen your mental muscle by actively challenging it. Don't put the puzzle book down when the solution is not immediately apparent. By testing your mind, you will discover the joy of a particular kind of accomplishment: watching your mental powers grow. You must have the feeling of mental effort and exertion in order to exercise your brain.

This brings us to the next issue. While all puzzles are good for you, the degree of their effectiveness as brain conditioners is not the same. Some puzzles test only your knowledge of facts. Such puzzles may be enjoyable and useful to a degree, but they're not as useful in conditioning your brain as the puzzles that require you to transform and manipulate information or do something with it by logic, multistep inference, mental rotation, planning, and so on. The latter

puzzles are more likely to give you the feeling of mental exertion, of "stretching your mind," and they are also better for your brain health. You can use this feeling as a useful, though inexact, assessment of a puzzle's effectiveness as a brain conditioner.

Try to select puzzles in a way that complements, rather than duplicates, your job-related activities. If your profession involves dealing with words (e.g., an English teacher), try to emphasize spatial puzzles. If you are an engineer dealing with diagrams, focus on verbal puzzles. If your job is relatively devoid of mental challenges of any kind, then mix several types of puzzles in equal proportions.

Cognitive decline often sets in with aging. It often affects certain kinds of memory, as well as specific aspects of attention and decision making. So it is particularly important to introduce cognitive exercise into your lifestyle as you age to counteract any possible cognitive decline. But cognitive exercise is also important for the young and the middle-aged. We live in a world that depends increasingly on the brain more than on the brawn. It is important to be sharp in order to get ahead in your career and to remain at the top of your game.

How frequently should you exercise your mind and for how long? Think in terms of an ongoing lifestyle change and

not just a short-term commitment. Regularity is key, perhaps a few times a week for 30 to 45 minutes at a time. We've tried to make this easier by offering a whole series of *Brain Games*™ books. You can carry these puzzle books—your "cognitive workout gym"—in your briefcase and shopping bag. Our puzzles are intended to be fun, so feel free to fit them into your lifestyle in a way that enhances rather than disrupts it. Research shows that even a relatively brief regimen of vigorous cognitive activity often produces perceptible and lasting effects. But as with physical exercise, the results are best when cognitive exercise becomes a lifelong habit.

To help you gauge your progress, we have included two self-assessment questionnaires: one at the beginning of the book and one after the last puzzle in the book. The questionnaires will guide you in rating your various cognitive abilities and any change that you may experience as a result of doing puzzles. Try to be as objective as possible when you fill out the questionnaires. Improving your cognitive skills in real-life situations is the most important practical outcome of exercising your mind, and you are in the best position to note such improvement and to decide whether or not it has taken place.

Now that you're aware of the great mental workout that awaits you in this book, we hope that you'll approach these puzzles with a sense of fun. If you have always been a puzzle fan, we offer a great rationale for indulging your passion! You have not been wasting your time by cracking challenging puzzles—far from it; you have been training and improving your mind.

So, whether you are a new or seasoned puzzle-solver, enjoy your brain workout and get smarter as you go!

ASSESS YOUR BRAIN

You are about to do something mentally challenging—that is, wrestle with a variety of puzzles to improve your mind. But before you start, take a few minutes to fill out this self-assessment questionnaire. It is designed to help you understand how your brain works before you tackle the puzzles in this second collection of *Brain Games*™. Then you will be able to track any changes in your mental performance and discover the ways in which you have improved.

The following questions will test your skills in the areas of memory, problem-solving, creative thinking, attention, language, and more. Please reflect on each question and rate your responses on a 5-point scale, where 5 equals "excellent" and 1 equals "very poor." Then tally up your scores and check out the categories at the bottom of the next page to learn how to sharpen your brain.

1. You're at a party, and you hit it off with someone who could be an important business contact. She gives you her phone number, but you don't have anything to write it down with. How likely are you to remember her phone number?

    1   2   3   ④   5

2. How good are you at giving people directions? Do you find that you can explain yourself clearly the first time, or do you frequently need to go back to the beginning and explain directions a different way?

    1   2   ③   4   5

3. Consider this situation: You're having a dinner party, and a guest calls at the last minute to ask if he can bring 4 friends who are visiting from out of town. How good are you at juggling your plans to accommodate this unanticipated change?

    1   2   ③   4   5

4. How well do you remember the locations of items you use every day, like your keys, cell phone, or wallet? When you need these items, can you locate them easily, or do you have to take time to search for them?

    1   2   3   4   ⑤

5. When you're reading a book or watching a movie, how good is your ability to concentrate? Deduct points if you're easily distracted.

    1   ②   3   4   5

6. At work, are you able to efficiently handle more than 1 project at a time, or do you have trouble devoting the necessary attention to each one?

1   2   3   4 (5)

7. You buy a new dresser, but assembly is required. When you look at the directions, you find that the illustrations have no written instructions. How good are you at deducing the instructions by interpreting the pictures?

1   2   3 (4) 5

8. When you go to the grocery store without a list, how good are you at remembering what you need? If you often forget essential items, deduct points accordingly.

1   2 (3) 4 5

9. How good are your everyday math skills? Are you able to add, subtract, multiply, and divide well in your head?

1   2 (3) 4 5

10. You receive a bill from your phone company that seems high, but the charges are broken down into complicated categories. You want to have a handle on all the charges before disputing the bill. How good are you at using logic to decipher your monthly statement?

1   2 (3) 4 5

10–25 Points:

Are You Ready to Make a Change?

Remember, it's never too late to improve your brain health! A great way to start is to work puzzles on a regular basis, and you've taken the first step by picking up this book. Choose a different type of puzzle each day, or do a variety of them to help strengthen memory, focus attention, and improve logic and problem-solving skills.

26–40 Points:

Building Your Mental Muscles

You're no mental slouch, but there's always room to sharpen your mind. Choose puzzles that will challenge you, especially the types of puzzles you might not like as much or would normally avoid. Remember, doing a puzzle can be the mental equivalent of doing lunges or squats: While they might not be your favorite activities, you'll definitely like the results!

41–50 Points:

View from the Top

Congratulations! You're keeping your brain in tip-top shape. To maintain this level of mental fitness, keep challenging yourself by working puzzles every day. Like the rest of the body's muscles, your brain can atrophy if you don't use it. So choose to keep your mind strong and active. You're at the summit—now you just have to stay fit to enjoy the view!

JUMP-START YOUR BRAIN

Screwprint: Tracing the Print

A screw is placed on a sheet of paper as shown in the illustration. Now, the screw rolls to the right along the sheet's edge. What imprint, from among A through E, would the screw threads produce on the small triangle shown in the middle of the sheet?

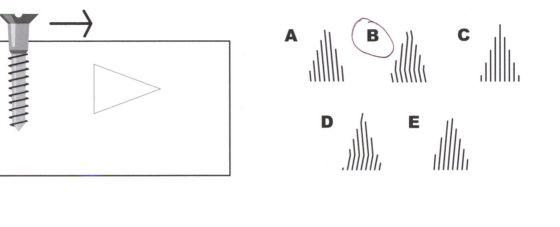

Hidden Names

Nine common first names are hidden in the sentence below. What are they?

ALABAMA RYE BREAD IS DANDY,

BUT ANGLOPHILES ARE USED TO

AUTOMAT TOAST.

*Al, Mary, Dan, Phil, Matt, Les, ED, TOM
Andy*

Answers on page 171.

Cat Got Your Dog?

LANGUAGE   **PLANNING**

Change CAT to DOG in 3 steps. Change just 1 letter on each line to go from the top word to the bottom word. Each line will contain a new word. Do not change the order of the letters.

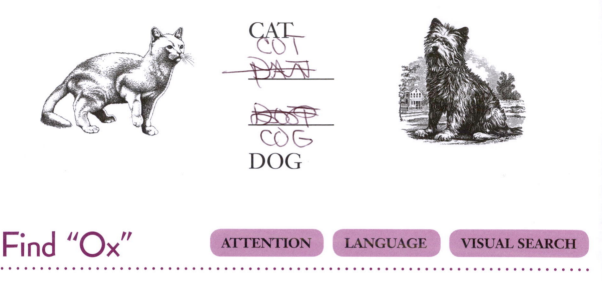

CAT
~~COT~~
~~DAT~~

~~DOOP~~
COG
DOG

Find "Ox"

ATTENTION   **LANGUAGE**   **VISUAL SEARCH**

Find all occurrences of the word "ox" in the paragraph below.

While working at Fort Knox, Otto Xavier put a box of rocks in Roxy's in-box, hoping to get her attention. Roxy found the box when she went to go Xerox the announcement that she was leaving Fort Knox to attend Oxford on a rowing scholarship as a coxswain. When he saw the announcement, Otto x-ed out Roxy's name in his Rolodex and turned his attention to Moxy, a foxy chatterbox he met at cardiokickboxing.

16

Answers on page 171.

12

How to Go Through a Stop Sign

Some prankster has taken an octagonal stop sign and painted a maze over it. The Traffic Fairy says it can be restored only if you can find the shortest way into the center. Hint: There is a bridge you can go under and over (where there is a line instead of a wall).

Answer on page 171.

Dry Your Eyes

Can you "read" the phrase below?   *Don't cry over spilled milk*

DON'T CRY

SPLASHED MILK

Three-Letter Anagrams

An anagram is a word made up of the rearranged letters of another word (as in *made* and *dame*). Fill in the blanks in each sentence below with words that are anagrams of one another.

1. The mama *ewe* was proud of her *wee* baby lamb.

2. Dad was disgusted to find a wad of *gum* at the bottom of his coffee *mug*.

3. *Pam* needed a *map* to find her friend's house.

4. Although it was very heavy, the bookcase did *not* weigh a *ton*.

5. It took *two* tugboats to *tow* the freighter into port.

6. *Deb* was so tired that she went right to *bed*.

Answers on page 171.

Do the Math

Use the clues to determine which of the digits 1 through 9 belongs in each square in the diagram. Digits may be repeated within a number, and no zeros are used.

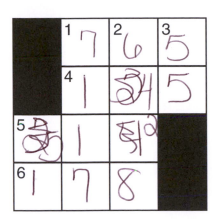

Across

1. Consecutive digits, descending
4. A multiple of 5
5. A perfect cube
6. Its last digit is the sum of its first 2 digits

Down

1. A palindrome
2. Consecutive even digits, in some order
3. A multiple of 11
5. A multiple of 3

Hint: The complete list of 3-digit perfect cubes is: 125, 216, 343, 512, 729.

First Assembling

Each of the 8 square tiles shown in the illustration contains some part of the number "1." Select the 4 tiles that together can create a 2×2 square so that a full "1" character appears on it. Tiles should not be rotated, flipped over, and/or overlapped.

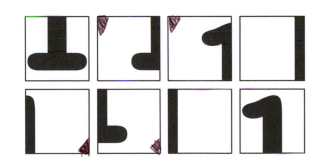

Answers on page 171.

Inherit the Win

Cryptograms are messages in substitution code. Break the code to read the message. For example, THE SMART CAT might become FVO QWGDF JGF if F is substituted for T, V for H, O for E, and so on. Hint: Look for repeated letters E, T, A, O, N, R, and I; OF, IS, and IT are common 2-letter words; THE and AND are common 3-letter words.

HZWLBW IBLK'D HOJQ TOK DS

FZXL RZDQ GOD DQLV HIUL PBLID

IKJLWDSBW.

Frequency of the coded letters:

A–0, B–4, C–0, D–7, E–0, F–1, G–1, H–3, I–4, J–2, K–3, L–7,

M–0, N–0, O–3, P–1, Q–3, R–1, S–2, T–1, U–1, V–1, W–4,

X–1, Y–0, Z–3.

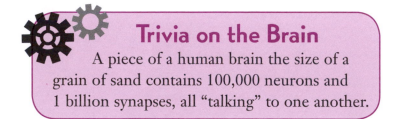

Trivia on the Brain

A piece of a human brain the size of a grain of sand contains 100,000 neurons and 1 billion synapses, all "talking" to one another.

Answer on page 171.

Yardful of Y's

The yard in this picture is full of things that begin with the letter "Y." We count 7.
How many different things that begin with a "Y" can you find?

Answers on page 171.

Rhyme Time: Fly By

Answer each clue below with a pair of rhyming words. The numbers that follow each clue indicate how many letters are in each word. For example, "what time sometimes seems to do" would be "fly by."

1. What time sometimes seems to do (3, 2): <u>FLY BY</u>

2. It's near the orchestra (3, 3): _____

3. Thirsty man's request (4, 4): _____

4. Pre-swim leaf remover (4, 4): _____

5. Farmer's lament after the rain (4, 5): _____

6. Coach's directive to the team (5, 4): _____

7. Where a beast of burden is trained (4, 6): _____

8. Where to learn to make hula skirts (5, 5): _____

9. Sweeping duty (5, 5): _____

10. It's said too softly (7, 4): _____

Passing a Bird's Home

Can you "read" the phrase below?

one flew
1FLU

over the cuckoos nest
CUCKOO'S HOME

Answers on page 171.

Times Across and Down

COMPUTATION   LOGIC

3				42
5				50
3				27
1				40

45 8 75 84

Here's a puzzle that will test your multiplication skills. Fill each square in the grid with a digit from 1 to 9. When the numbers in each row are multiplied, you should arrive at the total in the right-hand column. When the numbers in each column are multiplied, you should arrive at the total on the bottom line. Important: Any digit other than 1 may be repeated in a row or column. You will never repeat 1.

Hint: Some squares contain a 5 or a 7. Identify these first.

C-Dissection

PLANNING   SPATIAL REASONING

Using just your eyes, can you divide the shape below into 5 congruent parts? You can only "cut" along the lines of the grid. Shapes may be mirrored.

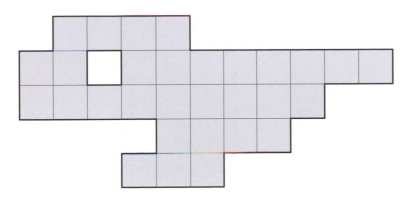

Answers on page 171.

It Figures

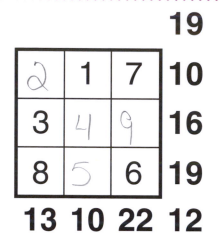

19

2	1	7	**10**
3	4	9	**16**
8	5	6	**19**

13 10 22 12

Fill each square in the grid with a digit from 1 to 9. When the numbers in each row are added, you should arrive at the total in the right-hand column. When the numbers in each column are added, you should arrive at the total on the bottom line. The numbers in each diagonal must add up to the totals in the upper and lower right corners.

Sudoku Fun

To solve a sudoku puzzle, place the numbers 1 through 9 only once in each row, column, and 3×3 box. Each puzzle has some numbers filled in—you just need to work out the rest. You'll never have to guess; each number can be found using the power of deduction.

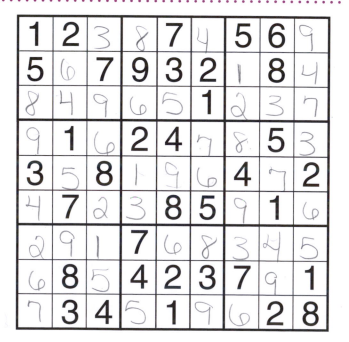

1	2	3	8	7	4	5	6	9
5	6	7	9	3	2	1	8	4
8	4	9	6	5	1	2	3	7
9	1	6	2	4	7	8	5	3
3	5	8	1	9	6	4	7	2
4	7	2	3	8	5	9	1	6
2	9	1	7	6	8	3	4	5
6	8	5	4	2	3	7	9	1
7	3	4	5	1	9	6	2	8

Answers on page 172.

Mirror—Pepper

There's no trick here, only a challenge: Draw the mirror image of these familiar objects. You may find it harder than you think!

ABCD Numbered

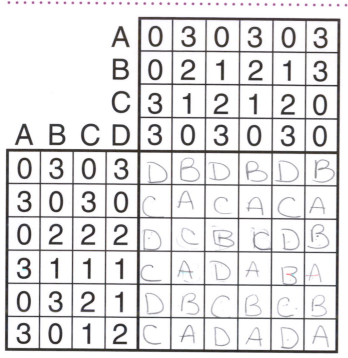

Every cell in this 6×6 grid contains one of the following 4 letters: A, B, C, or D. No letter can be horizontally or vertically adjacent to itself. The tables above and to the left of the grid indicate how many times each letter appears in that column or row. Can you complete the grid?

Good Fortune Maze

SPATIAL REASONING · PLANNING

Doesn't this maze look like a screen seen in Chinese restaurants? All you have to do in this maze is start at the top left and come out the bottom right as quickly as possible.

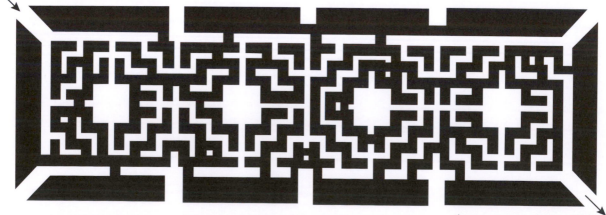

Answers on page 172.

Word Columns

To find the statement, put the letters that appear in the bottom half of the puzzle into the column of boxes above them. The letters may not be listed in the exact order in which they appear in the boxes. Mark off used letters below the grid. A letter may be used only once. The black boxes represent the space between words.

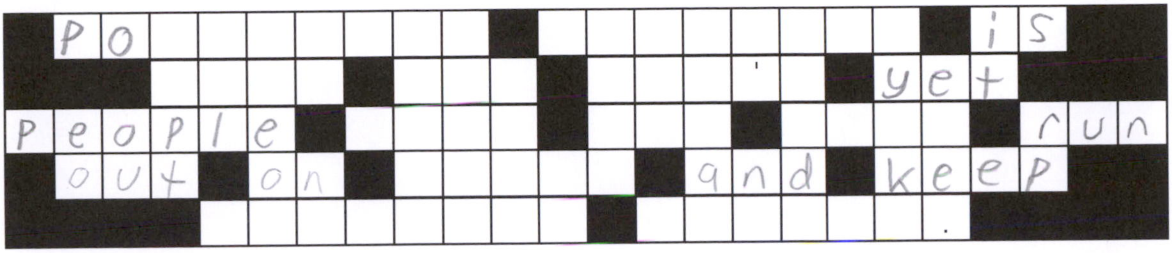

The grid (handwritten answers):

Row 1: P O [ ][ ][ ][ ]■[ ][ ][ ][ ][ ]■ i s
Row 2: ■[ ]■[ ]■[ ]■[ ][ ]' [ ]■ y e t ■
Row 3: P e o p l e ■[ ]■[ ][ ]■[ ][ ]■[ ][ ]■ r u n
Row 4: o u t ■ o n ■[ ][ ][ ]■[ ] a n d ■ k e e p
Row 5: ■[ ][ ][ ][ ][ ][ ]■[ ][ ][ ]■[ ] .

Letters below the grid:

```
        e       a   d               n       e       y
    l   l   o   i       t   o   u       y   a   a   d       y
e   u   p   i   e   n   c   y   i   e   a   t   r   n   y   t   a   l   e   t   p
P   o   t   s   h   o   u   n   o   w   g   s   o   a   n   h   g   k   e   e   s
p   o   o   w   h   t   f   k   i   l   n   s   d   o   u   t   w   a   v   e   i   r   u   n
```

In the Room

There's only one person in a room. Take some away, and there's still one in the room. Who is in the room?

Answers on page 172.

Life's Little Mysteries

LANGUAGE   LOGIC

Cryptograms are messages in substitution code. Break the code to read the message. For example, THE SMART CAT might become FVO QWGDF JGF if F is substituted for T, V for H, O for E, and so on.

Below are 5 questions we haven't quite figured out the answers to. The code is the same for each question.

1. BFZ ED WFJZ HCRR UW C WN LJW BFJM

   ZDO DMRZ KJW DMJ?

2. BFZ UL UW WFCW BFJM ZDO WICMLGDIW

   LDQJWFUMK YZ HCI, UW'L C LFUGQJMW,

   YOW BFJM ZDO LJME UW YZ LFUG, UW'L

   HCRRJE HCIKD?

3. FDB EDJL WFJ KOZ BFD EIUNJL WFJ

   LMDBGRDB KJW WD BDIA UM WFJ QDIMUMK?

4. HCM CM CQYUEJPWIDOL GJILDM QCAJ CM

   DVVFCME IJQCIA?

5. BFZ EDM'W WFJZ XOLW QCAJ VDDE LWCQGL

   JEUYRJ?

Answers on page 172.

Fly Away

Change just 1 letter on each line to go from the top word to the bottom word. Each line will contain a new word. Do not change the order of the letters.

DOVE

Love ____ profound affection

Lore ____ traditional knowledge

Lure ____ to tempt

Lurk ____ to wait secretly

LARK

The Hidden Shape

In the grid, find a stylized shape *exactly* like that shown next to the grid. The shape can be rotated but not mirrored.

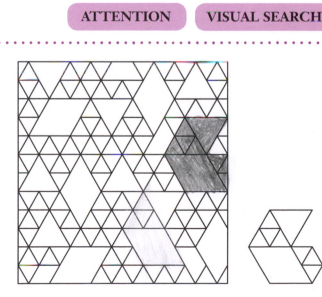

Answers on page 172.

Fitting Words with a G

In this miniature crossword, the clues are listed randomly and are numbered only for convenience. Figure out the placement of the 9 answers. To help you out, 1 letter is inserted in the grid, and this is the *only* occurrence of that letter in the completed puzzle.

Clues

1. Part of a book
2. Opposite of verbose
3. Cashews and almonds
4. Give a paddling to
5. Slightly open, as with a door
6. "Shoo!"
7. "...with a banjo on my _____"
8. Louisiana cuisine
9. Glass marble

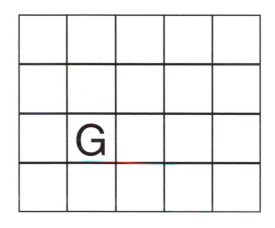

The Days Are Numbered

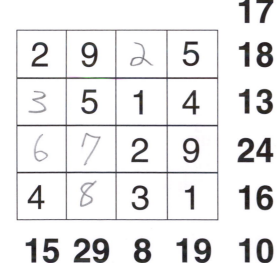

Fill each square in the grid with a digit from 1 to 9. When the numbers in each row are added, you should arrive at the total in the right-hand column. When the numbers in each column are added, you should arrive at the total on the bottom line. The numbers in each diagonal must add up to the totals in the upper and lower right corners.

Answers on page 172.

26

Number Quest

Put these pieces together to find a number in the middle. Visualize that number using your mind and eyes. Some pieces may be mirrored.

Trivia on the Brain

The frontal lobes of your brain create feelings of self-awareness. Evidence suggests that children develop self-awareness at around 18 months of age.

Answer on page 173.

Mosaic Maze

Don't let the squares confuse you. You can mosey from start to finish in a flash. Take the fastest route.

Trivia on the Brain
Your brain uses fatty acids from fats to create the specialized cells that allow you to think and feel.

Answer on page 173.

28

The Stars Are Numbered

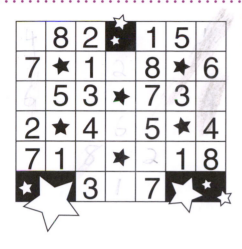

Fill each of the squares in the grid so that every star is surrounded by the digits 1 through 8 with no repeats.

Edible Anagrams

Fill in the blanks in each sentence below with words that are anagrams (rearrangements of the same letters) of each other.

1. Elizabeth kept a daily _diary_ and wrote about her trip to see the cows at the _dairy_ farm.

2. "I tried to wash off the _sauce_," said the cook, "but it was a lost _cause_."

3. "Go _forth_, young man," said the trail boss, as he was dipping into the cook's mulligan _froth_.

4. "At my _last_ checkup," said Sam, "the doc said I needed to cut down on _salt_."

5. At the pep talk to his losing _team_, the coach said, "You boys are looking a bit anemic. Eat some red _meat_!"

Answers on page 173.

Spin a Web

GENERAL KNOWLEDGE · LANGUAGE

Across

1. Splashy sound
5. Zoo gift from China
10. Fastener for a door
14. Adore
15. With the voice
16. Locale
17. Iridescent gemstone
18. Juliet's beau
19. Shopping center
20. Thoroughly cooked: hyph.
22. Wander widely
24. Created
25. Wise one
26. Like a killer's eyes
29. Mexican bulbous herb
33. Word before "wolly doodle"
34. Offspring
35. Triumph
36. Object of worship
37. Fry lightly and quickly
38. Color
39. Gentle touch
40. Valley _____
41. Schoolmate with a cap
42. Offensive sights
44. _____ than life
45. Versifier
46. Primary
47. Ghostly apparition
50. Nightly report
54. Ship section
55. Each and all
57. Table spread
58. Rim
59. Bridal path
60. Swear
61. Rip
62. Put off
63. Small mountain lake

Down

1. Do a farm task
2. Swinging stride
3. Egg-shape
4. In confusion and haste: hyph.
5. Mocking imitation
6. By one's self
7. Alaskan town
8. Payable
9. Charming and cute
10. Carpenter's tool
11. Spirited horse
12. Wall Street order
13. Pallid
21. Tyne or Tim
23. Matured
25. Connected hotel rooms
26. Petty malice
27. Now
28. Run away to wed

29. Hoodlums
30. Having debts
31. Then until now
32. Go in
34. Editor's mark
37. Disgruntled person
38. Renegade
40. 12 inches
41. Platform
43. Spinner of webs

44. Attorney
46. European blackbird
47. Sharpen
48. Traveled on horseback
49. Seaweed
50. Bird's home
51. Thomas _____ Edison
52. Prophet
53. Ripped
56. Compete

Answers on page 173.

Rhyme Time: Free Me

Answer each clue below with a pair of rhyming words. The numbers that follow each clue indicate how many letters are in each word. For example, "captive's plea" would be "free me."

1. Captive's plea (4, 2): <u>FREE ME</u>

2. Bargain in the produce section (4, 4): _____

3. Mailed a large monthly payment (4, 4): _____

4. Remains agreeable (5, 4): _____

5. Sign just before the turn (5, 4): _____

6. Excel at the bee (5, 4): _____

7. Trapper's backup (5, 5): _____

8. Restocking shelves, e.g. (5, 5): _____

9. Especially commonplace (5, 5): _____

10. Run-of-the-mill prom (6, 6): _____

It's Thrilling

Can you "read" the phrase below?

SUDDEN DEMISE

TIME

Answers on page 173.

Anagram Pairs

An anagram is a word made up of the rearranged letters of another word (as in *made* and *dame*). Fill in the blanks in each sentence below with words that are anagrams of one another.

1. Tiny bones _____ in the inner _____.

2. We had a _____ of mud on our boots from walking in the _____.

3. He's the only one _who_ knows _how_ to do the job.

4. The poet wrote an _ode_ to the _doe_ in the forest.

5. The angler caught _____ minnows with his _____.

6. The _____ sat on a _____ branch of the tree.

7. We were surprised that the _____ liked the green _____ soup.

8. _____ took a first _____ course at the hospital.

9. Dad woke up from his _nap_ when I dropped the tin _pan_.

10. The teaching _____ took the _____ to school.

Trivia on the Brain

Your amygdala is responsible for generating negative emotions such as anger, sadness, fear, and disgust. To be happy, that part of your brain must be kept quiet. Working on nonemotional mental tasks inhibits the amygdala, which is why keeping yourself busy can cheer you up when you're feeling down.

Answers on page 173.

Weather or Not!

Every word listed below is contained within this group of letters. Words can be found horizontally, vertically, or diagonally. They may read either backward or forward.

CLOUDY   SLEET

FLOOD   SNOW

HAIL   SUNNY

HURRICANE   TORNADO

RAIN   WIND

```
T  L  K  B  J  M  S  D  F
C  O  S  L  G  M  U  O  H
N  L  R  L  R  D  N  O  J
H  I  O  N  E  T  N  L  N
D  A  P  U  A  E  Y  F  I
L  H  L  W  D  D  T  W  A
S  N  O  W  M  Y  Q  I  R
H  U  R  R  I  C  A  N  E
Z  R  K  F  Y  T  K  D  N
```

One of the Dwarfs

Think of an expression to describe the picture on the left, and then rearrange the letters of this expression to form a 7-letter word. LLL, for example, is THREE L'S, whose rearranged letters form the word SHELTER.

Answers on page 173.

Spotted Flowers

Spring is here, and flowers are in bloom. But these flowers are spotted. How many dots can you find?

Animal Quest

PLANNING   SPATIAL REASONING

Put these pieces together to find an animal in the middle. Some pieces may be mirrored.

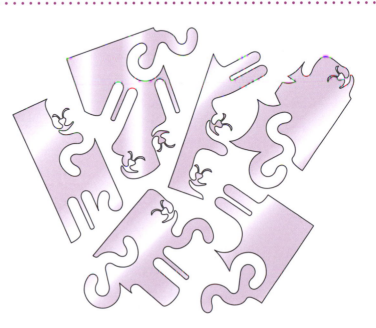

Answers on page 173.

Times Down and Across

COMPUTATION   LOGIC

Here's a puzzle that will test your multiplication skills. Fill each square in the grid with a digit from 1 to 9. When the numbers in each row are multiplied, you should arrive at the total in the right-hand column. When the numbers in each column are multiplied, you should arrive at the total on the bottom line. Important: Any digit other than 1 may be repeated in a row or column. You will never repeat 1.

Hint: Some squares contain a 5 or a 7. Identify these first.

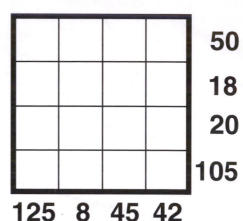

Squares Galore!

ATTENTION   VISUAL SEARCH

Don't be confused by the large squares! There are more squares than appear at first glance. How many can you count?

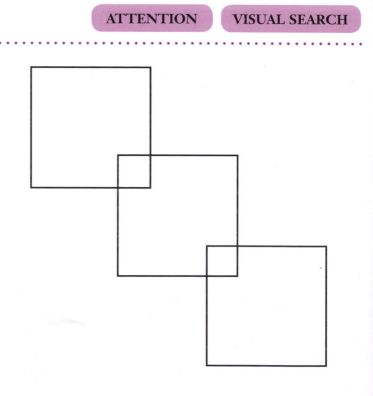

Answers on pages 173–174.

Bungle in the Jungle

The attentive hunter didn't plan for what he encountered in the jungle. It didn't take long for him to realize something was very wrong with the jungle and himself. We count 7 wrong things in this picture. How many can you find?

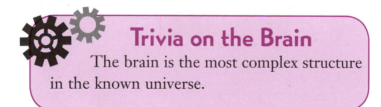

Trivia on the Brain

The brain is the most complex structure in the known universe.

Answers on page 174.

More Sudoku Fun

To solve a sudoku puzzle, place the numbers 1 through 9 only once in each row, column, and 3×3 box. Each puzzle has some numbers filled in—you just need to work out the rest. You'll never have to guess; each number can be found using the power of deduction.

5			6				7	8
			8				5	3
		3	1		4	2		
1	2	5	7				9	
4			8		5			2
	8				2	5	1	6
		2	9		1	3		
5	3			2				
7	9			4			2	

Trivia on the Brain

Why is your brain so soft? Ten percent of your brain is fat. This is because many of your brain's nerve fibers are wrapped in a fatty sheath. This fatty sheath, called *myelin*, is vital; it insulates the nerves. This allows electrical impulses to travel quickly around your brain.

Answer on page 174.

Fitting Words with an N

In this miniature crossword, the clues are listed randomly and are numbered only for convenience. Figure out the placement of the 9 answers. To help you out, 1 letter is inserted in the grid, and this is the *only* occurrence of that letter in the completed puzzle.

Clues

1. Sunburn soother
2. Great Barrier Reef material
3. Unaccompanied
4. Prepare for a trip
5. Slippery swimmers
6. Retains
7. Achy
8. Old hat
9. _____, Crackle, Pop

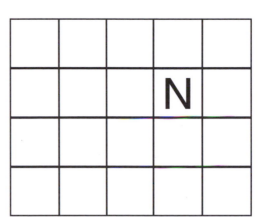

Odds-or-Evens

Rod and Steven play odds-or-evens throughout the week to decide who buys the beers after work on Friday. Winner gets a beer; loser buys. In a player's individual tally, however, 1 win and 1 loss cancel each other out (they keep a master tally on a bar napkin). When they arrive at the bar on Friday, the napkin shows that Rod has won 5 games of odds-or-evens but is getting no beers and has to buy Steven 4 of his favorite brews. How many games of odds-or-evens did they play that week?

Answers on page 174.

Rhyme Time: Why Fly

Answer each clue below with a pair of rhyming words. The numbers that follow each clue indicate how many letters are in each word. For example, "…when you can go by train?" would be "why fly."

1. "…when you can go by train?" (3, 3): <u>WHY FLY</u>

2. Question about wedding timing (3, 4): _____

3. Prepare anklets for shipping (3, 5): _____

4. Where most of the water goes out (4, 5): _____

5. Interrupt sleep increasingly (5, 4): _____

6. Heavyweight southpaw (5, 5): _____

7. Where big-ticket items are shown (5, 5): _____

8. Eric the Red's men (5, 5): _____

9. Barbecue that isn't used (5, 5): _____

10. Uncles (7, 8): _____

On Call

What is the missing letter in this sequence? Think of letters and numbers placed together.

A D G __ M P T W

Answers on page 174.

Season Search

ATTENTION **LANGUAGE** **VISUAL SEARCH**

Find the 4 names of the seasons. They may be found in any one of the 4 directions, written either across or down. No letter-card is used more than once.

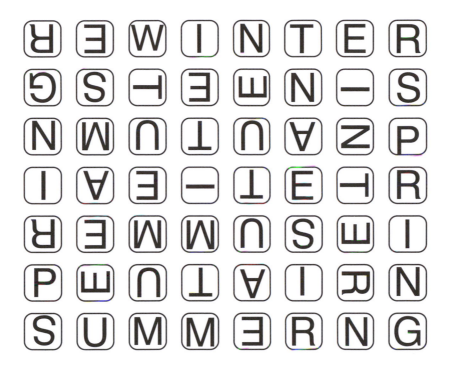

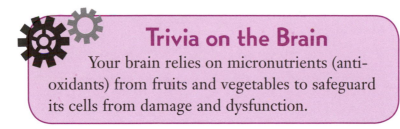

Trivia on the Brain

Your brain relies on micronutrients (anti-oxidants) from fruits and vegetables to safeguard its cells from damage and dysfunction.

Answer on page 174.

RECHARGE YOUR MIND

My Dinner with Andre

ATTENTION   **VISUAL SEARCH**

As with all films, there were some scenes in *My Dinner with Andre* that didn't work. This cut scene was the worst of them all. In fact, we find 11 things wrong with it. How many can you find?

Answers on page 174.

Head to Toes

LANGUAGE PLANNING

Change HEAD to TOES in 5 steps. Change just 1 letter on each line to go from the top word to the bottom word. Each line will contain a new word. Do not change the order of the letters.

HEAD

_____ to take in the meaning of written matter

_____

Toad small amphibian with rough, warty skin

_____

TOES

LANGUAGE

Go for the Gourd

ATTENTION VISUAL SEARCH

Find all occurrences of the word "go" in the following paragraph.

Gomer got the urge to drag out an orange gourd even though it wasn't Halloween. He carved his own face, which shows that his ego was a big one. Gomer got more gourds and carved a goose with gout, an egg on a wall, and a gang of gorillas going ape. He showed them to his gal Gloria, a former go-go dancer who was now a big old gourd grower from Georgia. She gave Gomer a bag of seeds to grow more gourds and go whole-hog out on his porch carving them.

Answers on page 174.

Food for Thought

Every word listed is contained in the group of letters below. The words can be found diagonally, and they may be read forward or backwaryd. The leftover letters spell a culinary message.

```
        E A C H C T T H W O R C
        D O R B S R O I R E A X
        W E P I I T A N U R R R
    E S F T H L S P R W B R R N U I O N
    I N A L T E U O O T O N M F C M Y C
    L O A R A R R G Z T H U E O R T M E
    U H O E S S G E A O L D F B I A N Y
    D H A U T N H N S O N F A S U G E E
    S B I R I F D I C T E E R Y L L H B
    B T I D D S O E N E H E L I S T A E
    S E D G T R L P B T V E S A A U K A
    H E R I C B O E U I H H B B Y U I W
    W S C Y R H A W N C P E E E D E O T
    R K I A N N E U T O Y G P Y E D R T
    H A M F S N E E U O N M T A T F I S
        A O C H N S O H T T T N
        Y I G D O P E A O P O E
        R O F C S J P A K E E N
```

bear fruit	go fish	Patty Duke
big cheese	hard row to hoe	Rice University
birthday suit	hot pursuit	rummy
carrot and stick	Johnny Reb	short list
coffee beans	marble column	sponge bath
crab nebula	not my cup of tea	wedding gown
English pound	oater	Where's the beef?
flash in the pan	ozone layer	

Answers on page 174.

Unmistakable Aroma

Cryptograms are messages in substitution code. Break this code to read the message. For example, THE SMART CAT might become FVO QWGDF JGF if F is substituted for T, V for H, O for E, and so on. Hint: This sentence contains a black and white animal.

SDE YJU'V JYV WKRI J AREUR

QKVGDEV ADCIDUI MIVVKUM

QKUT DL KV.

Play Sudoku

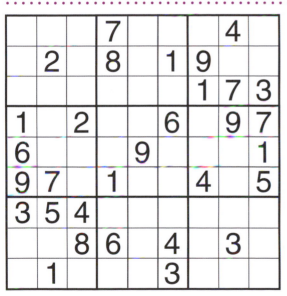

To solve a sudoku puzzle, place the numbers 1 through 9 only once in each row, column, and 3×3 box. Each puzzle has some numbers filled in—you just need to work out the rest. You'll never have to guess; each number can be found using the power of deduction.

Answers on pages 174–175.

Multiplicity

Fill each square in the grid with a digit from 1 to 9. When the numbers in each row are multiplied, you should arrive at the total in the right-hand column. When the numbers in each column are multiplied, you should arrive at the total on the bottom line. The numbers in each diagonal must multiply to total the numbers in the upper and lower right corners.

				135
4			5	240
5	4		2	120
	3	3		45
3	4		1	60
300	**192**	**135**	**10**	**48**

Dotted States

A lot of people live in Illinois, California, and Texas. This picture has filled these states with dots. How many can you find?

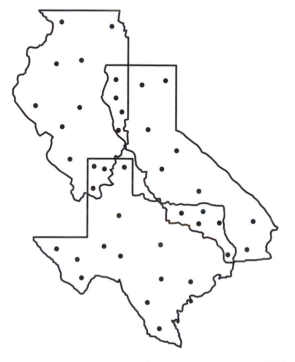

Answers on page 175.

H Is for Help!

Get from A to B as quickly as possible.

Like a Candy Bar

Can you "read" the phrase below?

CnHuOtCsK

Answers on page 175.

Records

Across

1. Estuaries
5. Brain waves
10. Absent
14. Seven-year problem
15. Goof
16. Miss: Sp.
17. Record: 3 wds.
19. Window part
20. Helix-wise
21. Precisely: 3 wds.
23. Baseball's Otis
24. To perfume
25. Described vividly
28. Fondler
31. Poem type
32. Paste-on
34. Move crab-wise
35. VIP's wheels, for short
37. Is intrepid
39. _____ me tangere: Lat.
40. Aerobatic thrills
42. Skewered morsel: var.
44. Victory
45. Flowed
47. Marsh birds
49. Pavlova and Magnani
50. Overstuff
51. Criticized
53. Shook
57. Took the bus

58. Records: 3 wds.
60. Burden
61. Leading
62. Beach sight
63. Grp. of voters
64. Mean
65. Featured one

Down

1. Tears
2. "Run _____ the flagpole…": 2 wds.
3. Play start: 2 wds.
4. Korean War navigating system
5. Blew inward
6. Tunes in
7. Catch sight of
8. Fruit punch
9. Mail machine
10. John Wilkes Booth
11. Records: 2 wds.
12. Norwegian personal name
13. Ivy League campus
18. Appointed
22. Individuals
24. Biblical spy
25. Lounges
26. Moron
27. Written record
28. Concerned
29. Little Eleanor

30. Wagon controls
33. Dessert choices
36. Candor
38. Church area
41. Rational
43. Cheer for the diva
46. Lunatic
48. Modifies

50. Thorax
51. Poke
52. Tops: hyph.
53. Schusses
54. Easy win
55. View from Taormina
56. Forest creature
59. _____ mode: 2 wds.

Answers on page 175.

Mirror—Goggles

There's no trick here, only a challenge: Draw the mirror image of these familiar objects. You may find it harder than you think!

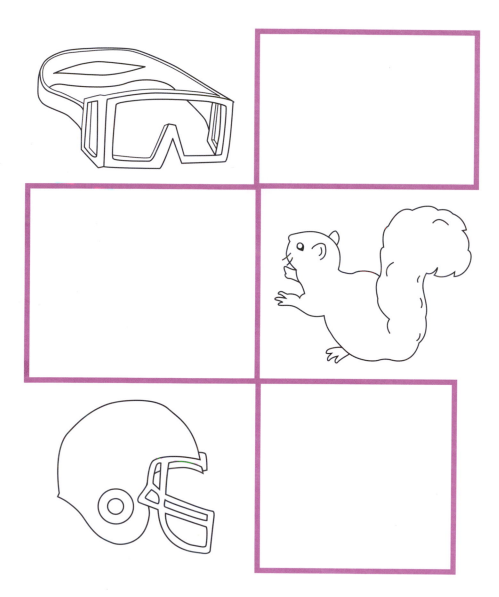

Rhyme Time: Imp Ump

Answer each clue below with a pair of rhyming words. The numbers that follow each clue indicate how many letters are in each word. For example, "he officiates over the little devils" would be "imp ump."

1. He officiates over the little devils (3, 3): IMP UMP

2. Fruity-flavored material for chewing (4, 3): _____

3. Hay (4, 4): _____

4. Where luges are stored (4, 4): _____

5. Shoe repairman's offering (4, 4): _____

6. Sovereign with nothing to do (5, 4): _____

7. Noble's work (5, 4): _____

8. Use too much adhesive (5, 5): _____

9. Lincoln/Douglas event of 1858 (5, 6): _____

10. Basis for a trucker's charge (7, 4): _____

Mind-Bender

We found this strange message carved on a rock in an ancient castle. Can you decipher it?

FLES TIFOM ARGAN ANASI ELF ITS

Answers on page 175.

Numbers in a Crossword

Use the clues to determine which of the digits 1 through 9 belongs in each square in the diagram. Digits may be repeated within a number.

Across

1. Consecutive digits, ascending
4. A perfect square
5. A perfect square
7. A multiple of 7

Down

1. The square root of 4–Across
2. A palindrome
3. Consecutive even digits, in some order
6. A perfect square

Hint: Start by noting that the last digit of 1–Down is the first digit of 4–Across.

Another Hidden Shape

In the grid, find a stylized shape *exactly* as that shown next to the grid. The shape can be rotated, but not mirrored.

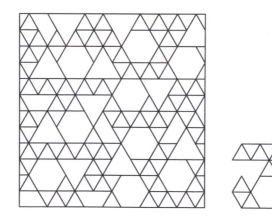

Answers on page 175.

Rhyming Duos

In this puzzle, we'll give you a phrase that sounds like a common pairing. For instance, "spam and legs" might remind you of "ham and eggs." Your mission: Match these strange duos with their common-phrase counterpart.

1. Skates and pleasures _____

2. Lax and lane _____

3. Cough and yawn _____

4. Whiz and spurs _____

5. Coarse and muggy _____

6. Wit and spun _____

7. Span and life _____

8. Last and moose _____

9. Court and feet _____

10. Clues and rocks _____

Special Number

What is special about this number?

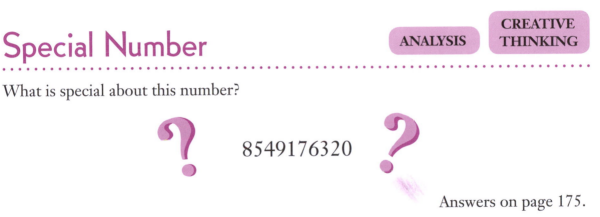

8549176320

Answers on page 175.

Caffeinated

Every word listed below is contained within this group of letters. Words can be found horizontally, vertically, or diagonally. They may read either backward or forward.

brew	O	Q	F	C	Y	S	U	G	A	R
cappuccino	N	O	S	S	E	R	P	S	E	L
coffee	I	N	M	L	A	T	T	E	F	E
cream	C	R	D	M	L	G	N	A	L	E
decaf	C	O	R	L	H	C	C	H	Q	F
espresso	U	A	M	W	M	E	G	K	M	F
latte	P	S	Q	O	D	A	N	K	B	O
mocha	P	T	R	L	C	F	E	R	J	C
roast	A	F	K	N	G	H	E	R	M	R
sugar	C	T	F	J	Q	W	A	K	C	T

Trivia on the Brain

Synesthesia is a curious condition in which there is a mingling of the senses due to cross-wiring in the brain. It occurs in about 1 out of every 2,000 people. For some people with synesthesia, hearing a musical note, for example, might cause them to see a particular color: C is red, F-sharp is blue. Or perhaps the number 2 is always green and 5 always yellow. Other people with the condition may taste spoken words: for example, on hearing the word "table," they might taste apricots, whereas "book" may taste like tomato soup.

Answers on page 175.

Word Columns

To find the statement, put the letters that appear in the bottom half of the puzzle into the column of boxes above them. The letters may not be listed in the exact order in which they appear in the boxes. Mark off used letters at the bottom. A letter may be used only once. The black boxes represent the space between words.

```
n     e o           l  e   n            h
 l  l s t     t s n c c e t i d      g t l e
 o b l e t s w a t c c y o l l t        O t h e
 c a c e u b m e h e o a r l u f t    w i o h s r
 s I c i a d i e i s d h i r a i e s I t t i f y
```

Back at You

Place it in a picture frame, and it shows a picture of you. Turn it upside down, and it still shows a picture of you right side up. What is it?

Answers on page 176.

Recharge Your Mind

From A to Z

CREATIVE THINKING **LANGUAGE**

Use every letter in the alphabet once to fill the blanks in this puzzle.

Dr. Don't-Dare!

ATTENTION **VISUAL SEARCH**

Things in the operating room have been crazy since the new doctor came to the hospital. We count 12 things wrong in this picture. How many can you find?

Answers on page 176.

Around the House

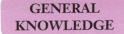

Level 2

GENERAL KNOWLEDGE **LANGUAGE**

This house-shape crossword is filled with—guess what?—stuff you'd find around the house. Since the letters don't intersect as in a conventional crossword, we've placed some letters in the house to help you solve the puzzle.

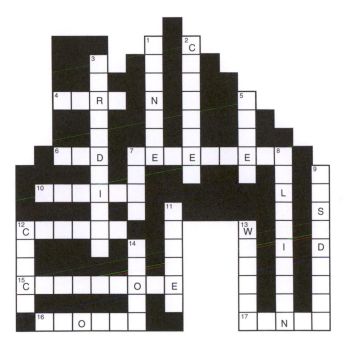

Across

4. It's found around the house
6. Night spot
7. All, for one
10. Sitters
12. Aladdin's vehicle
15. It usually gets a good talking to
16. Stills, maybe
17. Singer's asset

Down

1. Hot spot
2. It does Windows (more often than not)
3. Tool belt item
5. Type of tumbler
7. Pupil's place
8. Ernie Kovacs called it "a medium because it is neither rare nor well done"
9. Another word for "house"
11. Spillane's private eye
12. _____ potato
13. It's often found under a nut
14. Bibliophile's collection

Answers on page 176.

57

Times It!

Fill each square in the grid with a digit from 1 to 9. When the numbers in each row are multiplied, you should arrive at the total in the right-hand column. When the numbers in each column are multiplied, you should arrive at the total on the bottom row of numbers. Important: Any digit other than 1 may be repeated in a row or column. Hint: Consider the leftmost column first.

				126
				135
				70
				30

27 24 125 441

Triangles Within Triangles

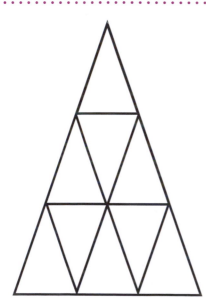

These triangles may point up. They may point down. How many triangles can you count?

Answers on page 176.

Word-Surfin' Safari

This story might seem to make sense, in a silly sort of way, but it makes even more sense if you're hunting for animals. They like to hide. If you're good at this, you might find as many as 25 of them here, "hidden in plain sight." They may be parts of words or stretched out across more than 1 word. (Some animals appear more than once, but they only count once. That's life in the jungle!) How many can you find?

Jack, a likable wizard, even if a bit of a craven coward, came looking for a pretty lass. He paced to and fro, getting more agitated by the moment. "This is a catastrophe!" he wailed. "The town is full of women, but which are the ones for me? They seem so standoffish." He rubbed the magic amulet on a leather strap around his neck. He wore it always, even when bathing. "I've got to go at it, just keep looking, but this is un-bearable! When will I find her?" He tried shouting his favor-ite magical incantations—"Banshee pickles!" and "Hairdress-er pentagon!" and "Bedlam boogie!"—but they had no effect at all. He didn't want his epitaph to read "Here Lies Jack, the Wizard of Lonely," he thought, popping a sad little Meal-for-

One of Slumgullion Stew into the microwave. Later, he took his dog, a beagle named Wolfgang, for a long walk. As Wolfgang stopped to leave his calling card with a fire hydrant, another dog appeared. Unlikely as it seemed, a comely owner was at the other end of its leash. Even more surprising, she had a friendly smile. The 2 dog-lovers got to chatting, and then, ever so casually, Jack found himself strolling along the sidewalk with his new acquaintance while their pets frolicked. Need we add that this comical farce had a happy ending?

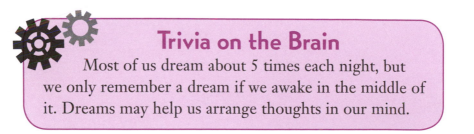

Trivia on the Brain

Most of us dream about 5 times each night, but we only remember a dream if we awake in the middle of it. Dreams may help us arrange thoughts in our mind.

Answers on page 176.

Find "Now"

Find all occurrences of the word "now" in the paragraph below.

During the snowstorm, Howard played Uno with Zowie, not knowing when the snowstorm would end. Unbeknownst to Howard, Zowie had no worries about winning because she knows how to palm Uno cards. Losing badly, Howard had a plan. "Ow!" he yelled, pretending to get a paper cut and sending the cards from Uno whirling to the floor. "Now you've done it," yelled Zowie, and she donned her snowshoes and left, knowing Howard had figured her out.

A Sudoku Treat

LOGIC

					3	6		
3			7	1		4		
5			8	4	6	2		
4	1			9				6
		5				1		
6				7			3	5
		3	4	8	1			7
		4		6	7			2
		6	9					

To solve a sudoku puzzle, place the numbers 1 through 9 only once in each row, column, and 3×3 box. Each puzzle has some numbers filled in—you just need to work out the rest. You'll never have to guess; each number can be found using the power of deduction.

Answers on page 177.

More Than a Word

Every word listed below is contained in the group of letters below. Words can be found diagonally and may read forward or backward.

```
        A S Y G C T B N O N T
        Y M F R R A O D O A R
        I S U R S O R H H N E
    L E G B D K E A A S T S V A C N T
    T H M E A R C H W T S U L O A E T
    M R O E U D C A U R L W A U N E A
    E I A N A I N O N G E R E I O N S
    L L N R N B E A S S C L I Y F S
    D E I R K A I R W E Y E R A G A O
    R I O F Y A L N C B V T D U R H M
    R O R R O A N L C I E N L E I E T
    P O R T T R O D S O O A N A T T H
    I O U I Y T P N F M M O R N S G E
    S L N G H R E W E I M E S S E B E
        G H F I U O M L I N S
        E F I L C O L A E C H
        O P B T C E H R A S E
```

base runner	crude oil	mean income	rough it
blue Monday	dirty rice	offensive line	salty snacks
coarse cloth	foul shot	Poor Richard	sorry about that
Common Era	gross weight	rank and file	Vulgar Latin
	low profile	raw recruit	

Answers on page 177.

In a Stew

It's dinnertime! Can you unscramble the ingredients for the stew?

RACTOR _____

RUPINT _____

ATASP _____

TOOTAP _____

SEINASONG _____

KELE _____

CENICHK _____

CRYLEE _____

Fire Figures

CREATIVE THINKING   LANGUAGE

Frank was the retiring fire chief at the Mathville Volunteer Fire Station, which has a number of firefighters who drive a number of fire trucks to fight fires. When his replacement showed up to take over, Frank decided to see how sharp the new man was. He told the new fire chief that if the firefighters at the station drive all the fire trucks to a fire, 1 firefighter doesn't get to drive. However, if they ride 2 to a fire truck, 1 fire truck gets left behind. The new chief proved he was worthy of the job by telling Frank the correct answer. How many firefighters work at the Mathville Station? How many fire trucks do they have?

Answers on page 177.

Bank Shot

LANGUAGE **LOGIC**

Cryptograms are messages in substitution code. Break this code to read the message. For example, THE SMART CAT might become FVO QWGDF JGF if F is substituted for T, V for H, O for E, and so on.

L CLS'W JCULSA WYR QGJWMERZ

JRZHLQR LS EU PCSD LJ PCV,

PGW XYRS L XRSW LS WYR MWYRZ

VCU CSV CJDRV WYR QKRZD WM

QYRQD EU PCKCSQR, JYR KRCSRV

MHRZ CSV IGJYRV ER.

X Marks the Spot!

COMPUTATION **LOGIC**

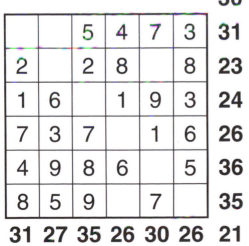

		5	4	7	3	**31**
2		2	8		8	**23**
1	6		1	9	3	**24**
7	3	7		1	6	**26**
4	9	8	6		5	**36**
8	5	9		7		**35**
31	**27**	**35**	**26**	**30**	**26**	**21**

30
31
23
24
26
36
35

Fill each square in the grid with a digit from 1 to 9. When the numbers in each row are added, you should arrive at the total in the right-hand column. When the numbers in each column are added, you should arrive at the total on the bottom line. The numbers in each diagonal must add up to the totals in the upper and lower right corners.

Answers on page 177.

Summertime Fun

¹	²	³	⁴		⁵	⁶	⁷		⁸	⁹	¹⁰ ¹¹

Across

1. Give up, as a territory
5. Nautical assent
8. Scottish girl
12. Get-out-of-jail cash
13. Drink like a kitten
14. Director Kazan
15. Summertime warmer
17. Waiter's handout
18. "Ouch!"
19. "On the Road" writer Jack

21. Restaurant bill, informally
23. Wish undone
25. Loosen, as a shoelace
26. Pole or Czech
28. Vintage photograph shade
30. Flower features
32. Make beloved
36. Kitchen gadget
38. Major show, briefly
39. Capital of Jordan
42. It precedes Sept.

64

44. Teacher's favorite
45. Knitted baby shoes
47. Major ISP
49. Play opener: 2 wds.
50. Summertime destination
54. "Scat!"
55. Priest's robe
56. By mouth
57. Merit
58. Put into service
59. Egg layers

Down

1. Cronkite's former employer
2. _____ de Cologne
3. Nutcake
4. "What _____ is new?"
5. "The Greatest" prizefighter
6. Northern Civil War soldier
7. Sporting blade
8. Summertime quaff
9. Native Alaskan
10. Mount in Exodus
11. Spaghetti topper
16. That girl
20. Wreck
21. Cookbook meas.
22. Pub offering
24. Cold War letters
27. Summertime respite from school
29. Lima's land
31. Unaccompanied

33. Emulate Christopher Columbus
34. Imitate
35. Deteriorate
37. Portrait painters' stands
39. Humiliate
40. Cocoa-flavored coffee
41. Car engine
43. Car fuel
46. Jacob's twin
48. "Yikes!": hyph.
51. Lincoln's nickname
52. Hightailed it
53. Golf legend Ernie

Answers on page 177.

Spinning in Circles

Connect the dots by finding the quickest way through this circular maze.

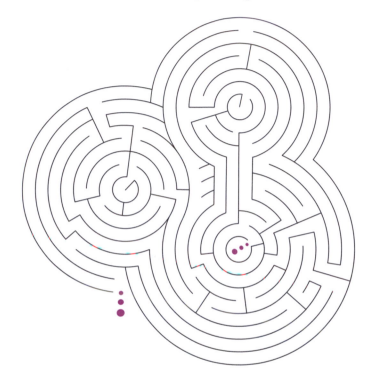

Begin Play

LANGUAGE

Can you "read" the phrase below?

HAND

SERVE

Answers on pages 177–178.

Rhyme Time: Wet Pet

GENERAL KNOWLEDGE   LANGUAGE

Answer each clue below with a pair of rhyming words. The numbers that follow each clue indicate how many letters are in each word. For example, "family friend fresh from the pool" would be "wet pet."

1. Family friend fresh from the pool (3, 3): <u>WET PET</u>

2. Ignore the underage gambling ban (3, 3): _____

3. It's created by hat removal (4, 4): _____

4. Approaching the bar (4, 4): _____

5. Amicable cheese-stealers (4, 4): _____

6. Enjoy an elegant meal (4, 4): _____

7. MD's foot cover (4, 5): _____

8. It's bottled in Germany (5, 4): _____

9. Pass around the wigs (5, 4): _____

10. Race postponement (5, 5): _____

Seasoned

ANALYSIS   CREATIVE THINKING

What is the next letter that gives flavor?

N A C __

Answers on page 178.

Thinking Outside the Bubbles

LANGUAGE

Rearrange the 4 groups of letters to form 1 word.

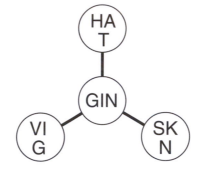

LOGIC

Fitting Words with an A

LANGUAGE   PLANNING

In this miniature crossword, the clues are listed randomly and are numbered only for convenience. Figure out the placement of the 9 answers. To help you out, 1 letter is inserted in the grid, and this is the *only* occurrence of that letter in the completed puzzle.

Clues

1. Wheel shaft
2. Born earlier
3. Banished person
4. Snow vehicle
5. His and _____
6. Catty comment?
7. Swampland
8. Unwanted plants
9. Take the bus

Answers on page 178.

Ticket to Ride

Congrats! You've been given a free airline ticket to an exotic country. But there's 1 little catch: You have to figure out what country. First, fill in the blanks according to the hints provided. Then unscramble the 9 letters in the center of each word to find out where you're headed. We've salted a few letters to give you a break.

1. Section in the delivery room? ...　＿＿ A ＿＿ | ＿＿ ＿＿ ＿＿ | ＿＿ A ＿＿

2. "Darning needle" ....　＿＿ ＿＿ A | ＿＿ ＿＿ ＿＿ | ＿＿ L ＿＿

3. Wristwatch, e.g ....　＿＿ I ＿＿ | ＿＿ ＿＿ ＿＿ | ＿＿ ＿＿ E

Unique Location

Black out 1 square so that there remains only 1 way to place the pentominoes into the grid. Pentominoes may be rotated and reflected.

Answers on page 178.

GEAR UP YOUR INTELLIGENCE

Ten-Five, Good Buddy

ATTENTION   **VISUAL SEARCH**

This wildcatter's been driving all night, and some strange things are happening. Is it all in his mind? Who knows? We count 9 things wrong with this picture. How many can you find?

Answers on page 178.

Sudoku Rules

LOGIC

To solve a sudoku puzzle, place the numbers 1 through 9 only once in each row, column, and 3×3 box. Each puzzle has some numbers filled in—you just need to work out the rest. You'll never have to guess; each number can be found using the power of deduction.

Go Forth and Multiply!

COMPUTATION   LOGIC

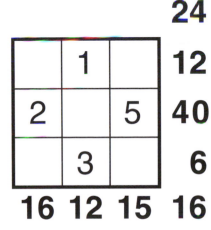

24

12

40

6

Fill each square in the grid with a single digit. When the numbers in each row are multiplied, you should arrive at the total in the right-hand column. When the numbers in each column are multiplied, you should arrive at the total on the bottom line. The numbers in each diagonal must multiply to total the numbers in the upper and lower right corners.

Answers on page 178.

Four-Letter Anagrams

An anagram is a word made up of the rearranged letters of another word (as in *made* and *dame*). Fill in the blanks in each sentence below with 4-letter words that are anagrams of one another.

1. Mom tried to _____ my brother to change his _____.

2. A car that needs an oil change can _____ lots of fumes in a short _____.

3. Drivers _____ to get very upset about a _____ in their fender.

4. The writer began to _____ when his _____ didn't get a prize.

5. _____ lives in Copenhagen and so is a _____.

6. The angler caught many _____, but nothing _____.

7. _____ of the streets were dark because there were so many _____ lights.

8. On an African map, the _____ looks like a long blue _____.

9. When someone embodies the wisdom of the _____, he is called a _____.

10. Since the _____ was too small, only _____ of the infield could be covered.

Travel Trouble

Bob and Rob are Siamese twins who always wanted to go on a vacation. Bob wanted to spend a week in Europe while Rob wanted to spend a week seeing the sights in China and Japan. Both left on the same day, returned 7 days later, and managed to fulfill their individual travel wishes. How did they do it?

Answers on page 178.

Zen in a Nutshell

LANGUAGE   LOGIC

Cryptograms are messages in substitution code. Break the code to read the message. For example, THE SMART CAT might become FVO QWGDF JGF if F is substituted for T, V for H, O for E, and so on.

HK NKXK TUC. HK YUSKVRGIK KRYK

RGZKX. OY ZNGZ YU IUSVROIGZKJ?

Triangles Galore!

ATTENTION   VISUAL SEARCH

Triangles are pointed in every direction. How many can you count?

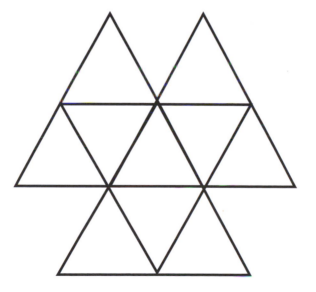

Answers on page 178.

73

Fitting Words with an M

In this miniature crossword, the clues are listed randomly, and the clues are numbered only for convenience. Figure out the placement of the nine answers. To help you out, one letter is inserted in the grid, and this is the *only* occurrence of that letter in the completed puzzle.

Clues
1. Love
2. Campus area
3. Conflagration
4. Like some stadiums
5. Computer "oops" command
6. Molecule part
7. Drink heartily
8. Ran away
9. Up to

The grid contains the letter **M** in the fourth row, second column.

So Many Books

LANGUAGE PLANNING

Change just 1 letter on each line to go from the top word to the bottom word. Each line will contain a new word. Do not change the order of the letters.

READ

_____

_____

_____

BOOK

Answers on page 178.

A Matter of Faith

Every word listed below is contained within this group of letters. Words can be found horizontally, vertically, or diagonally. They may read either backward or forward.

Baptist

Buddhist

Catholic

Hindu

Jewish

Lutheran

Methodist

Muslim

Protestant

Taoist

V	M	N	A	R	E	H	T	U	L	V	Y	M
B	X	J	R	C	G	X	R	B	M	J	B	T
F	U	T	A	O	I	S	T	W	L	E	G	T
T	N	D	H	M	Z	G	N	T	C	W	S	S
M	N	V	D	B	B	T	V	A	F	I	D	I
C	B	A	T	H	H	R	T	D	T	S	M	D
P	M	N	T	L	I	H	W	P	Q	H	P	O
D	U	F	G	S	O	S	A	W	M	F	L	H
N	D	J	T	L	E	B	T	I	X	L	C	T
T	N	J	I	V	Q	T	L	D	V	G	R	E
T	I	C	C	Y	X	S	O	B	G	H	W	M
T	H	R	H	R	U	K	K	R	G	X	T	K
M	D	M	L	M	Y	M	W	K	P	M	M	R

Trivia on the Brain

While you sleep, your brain is still active. When you dream, your brain is as active as it is when you are awake.

Answers on page 179.

Creature Corner

Across

1. Type of frost
5. Become prevalent: 2 wds.
10. _____ Hari
14. Ticklish creature
15. Relatives of 18–Across
17. Store div.
18. Gulf Coast reptiles
19. Type of dict.
20. Catalpa, for 1
21. NFL's Dilfer or Green
22. *Peer Gynt* dancer
24. Peep show
27. Under-the-table money
29. Lush and green
33. "Drinks on the house," for 1
35. Missing elements
37. Old card game
38. Horizon sight at Brighton
39. Dactyl preceder
40. Pot: Sp.
41. Advice columnist Landers
42. Merry sprees
43. Offspring
44. Conquer Everest anew
46. Dueling weapons
48. Supplied with weapons
50. Make a connection
53. Set free
56. Revise
58. Form. Middle East alliance
59. Armor-plated mammals
62. Kingston group size
63. Paleozoic arthropods
64. Followers of Attila
65. Superlative endings
66. Aquatic mammal
67. Alberto Azzo II was the first

Down

1. Ibsen role
2. New York city
3. Newt, frog, et al.
4. Balderdash
5. Pyramid insect
6. _____ Stanley Gardner
7. Sidney who played Chan
8. Here: Fr.
9. Holiday concoction
10. Fitted, like a joint: Brit.
11. Lily plant
12. Sea sight
13. Exec.'s aide
16. Those who see each other
20. Shipshape
23. Pony pace
25. Disinclined
26. Make over
28. Chateaubriand, e.g.
30. Its name means "other lizard"
31. _____ contendere: Lat.
32. One of 3–Down
33. Construction unit: hyph.
34. Accomplished

36. Cartoon cry
39. Sunday or Springs preceder
40. Soviet city
42. Western cattle town
43. Borscht ingredient
45. Memorable cellist
47. Finicky
49. River conclusion
51. Disgrace

52. Having an irregular, notched edge
53. Behind time
54. Hockey player Bobby et al.
55. Leave out
57. Activist
60. Nigerian native
61. Turned on a lamp
62. "_____ End"

Answers on page 179.

Family Vacation

LANGUAGE

ATTENTION   VISUAL SEARCH

Every word listed below is contained within this group of letters. Words can be found horizontally, vertically, or diagonally. They may read either backward or forward.

```
R   E   S   E   R   V   A   T   I   O   N   S   S
R   D   X   R   M   V   R   R   C   V   D   N   I
M   J   E   B   E   F   N   R   Q   T   Q   E   G
T   H   O   T   E   L   B   Z   R   K   L   E   H
M   L   B   R   S   L   A   O   X   D   F   R   T
P   L   R   A   N   U   P   T   E   M   X   C   S
L   B   K   C   T   R   A   L   I   T   V   S   E
A   T   H   L   I   T   A   H   R   V   G   N   E
N   L   R   A   R   Y   W   C   X   T   E   U   I
E   H   L   T   S   B   D   R   V   E   F   S   N
G   J   Y   N   P   N   C   X   G   N   K   S   G
S   T   N   E   M   U   G   R   A   J   A   F   C
E   X   W   R   N   K   B   G   J   G   L   T   P
```

airport	gas	rental car
arguments	hotel	reservations
delays	plane	sightseeing
exhausted	relatives	sunscreen

Answers on page 179.

Rhyme Time: Slow Flow

GENERAL KNOWLEDGE   **LANGUAGE**

Answer each clue below with a pair of rhyming words. The numbers that follow each clue indicate how many letters are in each word. For example, "plumbing problem" would be "slow flow."

1. Plumbing problem (4, 4): <u>SLOW FLOW</u>

2. Entrée option (4, 4): _____

3. Go on a road trip (4, 4): _____

4. Single objective (4, 4): _____

5. Bovine that just ate (4, 4): _____

6. "Jack and Jill" (4, 4): _____

7. Trumpeter's old instrument (4, 4): _____

8. Base-stealer's maneuver (4, 5): _____

9. Spectral party-giver (5, 4): _____

10. The "and" after "Four score" (5, 4): _____

11. Equine army (5, 5): _____

12. Pronouncement by U.S. Immigration (6, 5): _____

13. More irate snake (6, 5): _____

14. Improved epistle (6, 6): _____

15. Stronger snub (6, 8): _____

Answers on page 179.

Circular Reasoning

To solve this maze, just imagine you're on 1 of those survival-type shows. Your team and your rival team have been led, blindfolded, to the center. Now the blindfolds are off, and you have to find your way out. The team that negotiates this puzzle fastest wins. How soon can you get out?

How's the Weather?

What is the missing letter in this sequence of initial letters? Hint: Think of a European country.

TRISFM _ TP

Answers on page 179.

World Capitals

Cryptograms are messages in substitution code. Break this code to read the message. For example, THE SMART CAT might become FVO QWGDF JGF if F is substituted for T, V for H, O for E, and so on.

1. FUBF, HFKSIT

2. URFMPEFBD, USOAOH

3. HOS AOBEN, NHANI

4. MINKF, OLTJR

5. COBLKIAO, UOKCNI

6. IDUROKAID, HOREOKBIHAU

7. DIAKNA, UJINH

8. RFPTF, GIJIH

9. UIHRNILF, MENBO

10. JEHFD JOHE, MIDCFANI

Answers on page 179.

Mirror—Skateboard

There's no trick here, only a challenge: Draw the mirror image of these familiar objects. You may find it harder than you think!

Tricky Codeword Puzzle

Every number corresponds to a different letter—try to fill in the grid and deduce the words to crack the code!

1	2	3	4	5	6	7	8	9	10	11	12	13	14	15	16	17	18	19	20	21	22	23	24	25	26
P								M				A													

Words in the Puzzle:

adhere

amp

bet

bowl

earth

ever

exhibit

exploration

fear

fourth

handicap

ignored

images

mention

more

novelty

quoting

recognition

shouting

supporter

tidy

timing

tree

Answers on page 179.

83

Sittin' on Top of the World

Cover the questions on the next page while you read the following story. Then, after you read the story, cover it and answer the questions.

"On top of the world" is a great metaphor for being happy, but if you're literally on top of the world, let's hope you have a warm parka—it's cold up there! The top of our world is the Arctic, the northernmost region of Earth. It centers on the North Pole.

The Arctic area includes parts of 8 nations: Canada, Denmark (Greenland/territory), the United States, Russia, Finland, Iceland, Sweden, and Norway. The Arctic Ocean is the smallest of the world's 5 oceans and the shallowest. (The other 4 oceans are the Pacific, Atlantic, Indian, and Southern.) The Arctic is home to 2 million people who speak some 50 languages.

A treeless, frozen ground called "tundra" surrounds the Arctic region, which is mostly a huge, icy ocean. It sounds inhospitable, yet the Arctic teems with life. Fish and birds are abundant, and there are many land and sea animals, plus human communities. Animals include the polar bear, Arctic fox and Arctic hare, caribou (large deer also called reindeer), Dall sheep, the muskox, wolverine, and lemming. Marine mammals include whales, walruses, seals, and dolphins. Among the most curious animals is the narwhal, a whale with a tusk that can be 3 to 10 feet long. In that vast, empty-looking wilderness, there's a lot going on!

Questions:
1. The treeless, frozen ground of the Arctic is called (a) ice mass (b) tundra (c) lichen.
2. True or false: The Arctic region includes northern Estonia.
3. The northernmost part of the Earth is the (a) Antarctic (b) Acrostic (c) Arctic.
4. True or false: The official language of the Arctic is English.
5. Being "on top of the world" means you're (a) happy (b) melancholy (c) 50 miles up.
6. The central point of the Arctic is (a) the North Pole (b) the South Pole (c) the flagpole.
7. True or false: Greenland is a Danish territory.
8. The Arctic Ocean is the (a) biggest (b) shallowest (c) deepest ocean.
9. True or false: The narwhal is a type of walrus.
10. A caribou is a kind of (a) sheep (b) cardigan (c) large deer.

Star Power

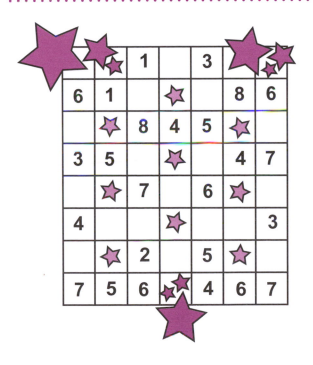

Fill each of the squares in the grid so that every purple star is surrounded by the digits 1 through 8 with no repeats.

Answers on page 180.

Spotted Tools

It's time to find your tools. But wait! They're full of dots. How many dots can you find?

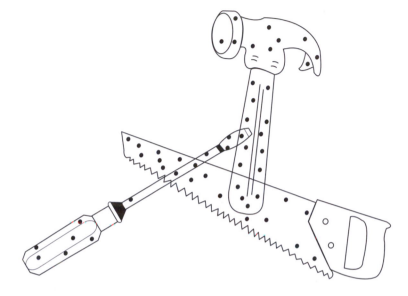

ABCD Challenge

COMPUTATION   LOGIC

Every cell in the 6×6 grid contains 1 of the following 4 letters: A, B, C, or D. No letter can be horizontally or vertically adjacent to itself. The tables above and to the left of the grid indicate how many times each letter appears in that column or row. Can you complete the grid?

				A	1	3	0	3	1	1
				B	3	1	1	1	3	0
				C	0	2	2	0	2	3
A	B	C	D	D	2	0	3	2	0	2
3	2	0	1	B						
2	1	2	1							
1	0	2	3							
1	2	2	1							
0	1	2	3							
2	3	1	0							

Answers on page 180.

Gaggle of G's

ATTENTION   **VISUAL SEARCH**

Within this picture is a gaggle of G's. We count 15 things beginning with the letter "G." How many can you find?

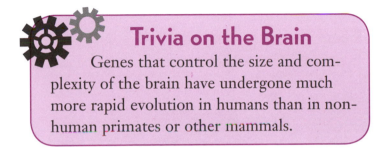

Trivia on the Brain

Genes that control the size and complexity of the brain have undergone much more rapid evolution in humans than in non-human primates or other mammals.

Answers on page 180.

Rules of Thumb

Cryptograms are messages in substitution code. Break this code to read the message. For example, THE SMART CAT might become FVO QWGDF JGF if F is substituted for T, V for H, O for E, and so on. The code is the same for each number.

1. GQGPYL: WQG NOM GCMZFV PWMYJFL OJG GQGPYL WU WQG ZKGPZYG IZQHL NZP WP WQG NFMG-OSD RWWHGQ XZOIJ.

2. DWTGP PMFG: FWWT ZPWMQH OJG OZNFG ZQH USQH OJG KSIOSX. SU LWM IZQ'O OGFF RJW SO SV, SO'V LWM.

3. JWR OW XSA Z DPWDGP WSF-ZQH-KSQGYZP VZFZH HPGVVSQY: OJPGG DZPOV WSF, WQG DZPO KSQGYZP.

4. RJZO OW NPSQY OW VMXXGP IZXD: Z YWWH PMFG WU OJMXN? SU LWM IZPG ZNWMO OJG SOGX, FGZKG SO ZO JWXG.

Sleigh Bells

Can you determine the missing letter in this logical progression?

D D P V C __ D B

Answers on page 180.

Why Oh Why Do I Multiply?

COMPUTATION   LOGIC

					16
		4	3	1	192
5	4			1	120
3	3		2	5	180
5		2		5	100
4	3		1		120
1200	144	240	24	50	128

Fill each square in the grid with a single digit. When the numbers in each row are multiplied, you should arrive at the total in the right-hand column. When the numbers in each column are multiplied, you should arrive at the total on the bottom line. The numbers in each diagonal must multiply to total the numbers in the upper and lower right corners.

Chill!

LANGUAGE   PLANNING

Change WARM to COLD in 4 steps. Change just 1 letter on each line to go from the top word to the bottom word. Each line will contain a new word. Do not change the order of the letters.

WARM

_____

_____

_____

COLD

Answers on page 180.

Deli Misadventures

GENERAL KNOWLEDGE   LANGUAGE

Across

1. Greek letter
4. Raised eyebrow shape
8. "Look what I did!": hyph.
12. "You've Got Mail" co.
13. Hide a treasure, maybe
14. All over again
15. "Were you puzzled over what to buy at the deli?": 5 wds.
18. Clear the windshield
19. Like a docked yacht
20. Sheepish remark?
22. Schuss
23. Somebody special
26. Martinique, *par exemple*
28. Like a wildly colored tie
32. "How would you describe the deli's decor?": 2 wds.
36. Menial worker
37. Pitcher's stat.
38. British explorer John
39. Participate in an auction
42. Fashion monogram
44. Nudged rudely
48. Chars
52. "And the proprietor? What was he like?": 3 wds.
54. Gait at the track
55. Skin lotion ingredient
56. Beachgoer's quest, often
57. Darns socks, maybe
58. Clucks disapprovingly
59. Wrath

Down

1. Bookie's worry
2. Sewing machine inventor Elias
3. Norwegian saint and king
4. First name of the second first lady
5. Stocking annoyance
6. Grouch
7. Publicizes, slangily
8. Perceptible to touch
9. Cross with a loop
10. Remove from text
11. Bowled over
16. Weep out loud
17. Vex
21. Everything
23. Big mouth
24. Have bills to pay
25. Tabloid tpc.
27. Give the once-over
29. Anthem contraction
30. Red, white, and blue letters
31. Turn red, perhaps
33. Opens, as a barn door
34. Weep
35. Big bothers
40. ___ Jima
41. Skim, as milk

43. Name of 13 popes
44. Young newts
45. Tackle box item
46. Totally botch
47. Bb. 2-baggers
49. Not pro
50. Paddler's target
51. Word in a New Year's Eve song
53. "All systems go" to NASA

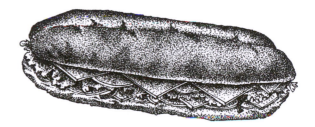

Answers on page 180.

Sudoku Rules Once More

To solve a sudoku puzzle, place the numbers 1 through 9 only once in each row, column, and 3×3 box. Each puzzle has some numbers filled in—you just need to work out the rest. You'll never have to guess; each number can be found using the power of deduction.

	1							
3	6			2	8			
		4	5				6	9
1	8				7			
2			8		6			3
			3				8	7
9	5				4	7		
			6	5			9	2
							5	

Easy as ABC

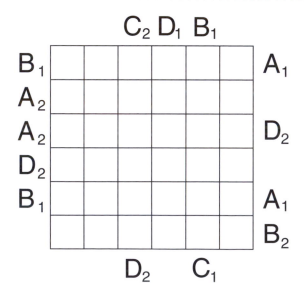

Each row and column contains A, B, C, D, and 2 blank squares. Each letter and number indicator refers to the first or second of the 4 letters encountered when traveling inward. Can you complete the grid?

Answers on pages 180–181.

Word Columns

To find the statement, put the letters that appear in the bottom half of the puzzle into the column of boxes above them. The letters may not be listed in the exact order in which they appear in the boxes. Mark off used letters at the bottom. A letter may be used only once. The black boxes represent the space between words.

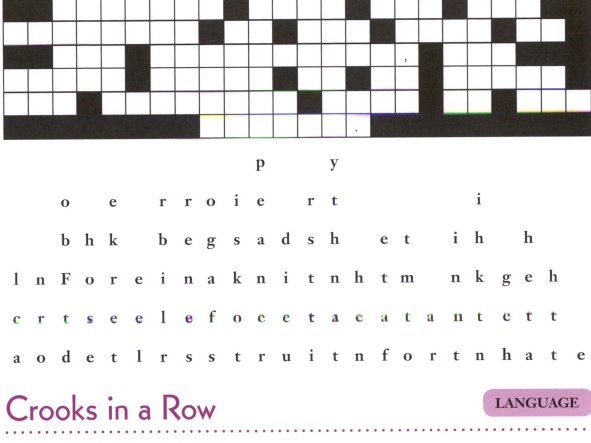

```
                    p           y

      o     e     r   r   o   i   e     r   t                 i

      b   h   k     b   e   g   s   a   d   s   h     e   t     i   h     h

  l   n   F   o   r   e   i   n   a   k   n   i   t   n   h   t   m     n   k   g   e   h

  c   r   t   s   e   e   l   e   f   o   c   e   t   a   e   a   t   a   n   t   e   t

  a   o   d   e   t   l   r   s   s   t   r   u   i   t   n   f   o   r   t   n   h   a   t   e
```

Crooks in a Row

Can you "read" the phrase below?

POLICE

N

I

L

Answers on page 181.

Play Ball!

Every word listed below is contained within this group of letters. Words can be found horizontally, vertically, or diagonally. They may read either backward or forward.

```
T  S  G  R  H  O  M  E  R  U  N  X
R  M  T  H  E  M  O  H  M  E  H  H
E  N  A  R  R  T  D  T  V  H  Y  X
H  W  W  L  I  N  N  I  N  G  V  W
C  A  M  G  S  K  R  H  C  Z  Q  R
T  L  N  R  B  D  E  E  R  K  R  R
I  K  T  X  E  T  N  S  O  B  R  D
P  H  V  N  Z  H  E  A  R  U  B  R
Y  P  I  F  F  V  C  B  R  A  T  K
H  L  M  L  O  B  Z  T  S  G  H  H
M  C  N  L  U  M  P  E  A  F  Y  F
Z  M  G  M  L  R  S  H  Q  C  Z  F
```

base hit	grand slam	out
bases	home	pitcher
catcher	home run	strikes
foul	inning	walk
glove	line drive	

Answers on page 181.

Get Smart!

LANGUAGE

Unscramble the words listed below. Then unscramble the marked letters to find a phrase that fits in the bottom row of boxes—a phrase that describes the listed words.

RARDBAN

NYRB RAWM

TUNMO KOLHOEY

LIEFCFRDA

TSMIH

RAASSV

WEYLLELSE

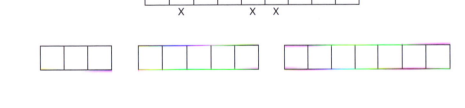

Vitamin Vic

CREATIVE THINKING   LOGIC

As Vitamin Vic pushes his grocery cart through the produce section, you observe that he picks up cucumbers but not lettuce. He grabs a zucchini but not asparagus. He picks up peas but no onions. Now he's approaching the cabbage and potatoes. Based on his previous selections, which one will Vic choose?

Answers on page 181.

President's Maxim

Cryptograms are messages in substitution code. Break the code to read the message. For example, THE SMART CAT might become FVO QWGDF JGF if F is substituted for T, V for H, O for E, and so on.

REP HLA MEEF OEKC EM UBC GCEGFC LFF EM

UBC UNKC, LAJ LFF EM UBC GCEGFC OEKC EM

UBC UNKC, DPU REP HLAAEU MEEF LFF EM UBC

GCEGFC LFF EM UBC UNKC.

—LDILBLK FNAHEFA

Trivia on the Brain

During childhood years, the brain can rewire itself to make up for many defects and injury. Unfortunately, as we age, this task becomes more difficult for our brains to complete.

Answer on page 181.

Rhyme Time: Soft Loft

Answer each clue below with a pair of rhyming words. The numbers that follow each clue indicate how many letters are in each word. For example, "hay-filled upper barn area" would be "soft loft."

1. Hay-filled upper barn area (4, 4): <u>SOFT LOFT</u>

2. NFL training camp defense exercise (4, 5): _____

3. Have too light of a color (4, 5): _____

4. It's right at the bottom (4, 5): _____

5. Praise a seasoning (5, 4): _____

6. It's wiped off after gluing (5, 5): _____

7. Where a blackbird is safe (5, 5): _____

8. Bakery byproduct (5, 5): _____

9. A rag for cleaning up soup spills (5, 5): _____

10. Thrive as an inventor (6, 5): _____

11. Move the cattle to a new pasture (6, 5): _____

12. He's using the middle of the mall (6, 6): _____

13. Holding place for some jewelry (6, 6): _____

14. A leash made from animal skin (7, 6): _____

15. Buyer born in 1950 (6, 8): _____

Answers on page 181.

NASCAR Family

LANGUAGE

SPATIAL PLANNING

Find a place in the grid for each of the words listed below.

3 Letters

ape	err	tot	dote
can	its	URI	Erma
emu	Nin	**4 Letters**	hope
Eno	sop	a lot	lyre
ere	ton	arch	oh no
ERN	top	chat	one-a

Pete
sits
smee
Sosa
test

5 Letters

Emile
Euros
intro
meals

mused
shunt

6 Letters

Apollo
citric
divert
dusted
hot air
mallet
missal

oriole
Reiner
retire
smeary
stupor
tenses
unholy

7 Letters

Anaheim
connive

decants
elision
records
Stiller
Toronto

8 Letters

doctoral
tea party

13 Letters

race relations

Solve Logidoku

The numbers 1 through 8 should appear once in every row, column, long diagonal, irregular shape (indicated by marked borders), and 2×4 grid (indicated by shaded or white blocks). With the help of the provided numbers in this square, can you complete the puzzle?

Answers on page 181.

It's a Wrap!

Which one of the cubes is a correct wrap of the center pattern?

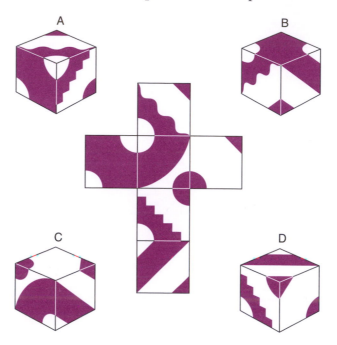

Numbered Stars

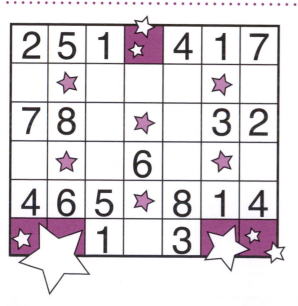

Fill each of the squares in the grid so that every purple star is surrounded by the digits 1 through 8 with no repeats.

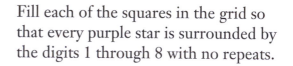

Answers on page 181.

And in Summary

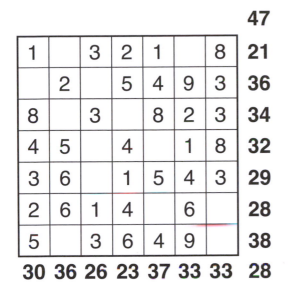

								47
1		3	2	1		8		21
	2		5	4	9	3		36
8		3		8	2	3		34
4	5		4			1	8	32
3	6		1	5	4	3		29
2	6	1	4		6			28
5		3	6	4	9			38
30	36	26	23	37	33	33	28	

Fill each square in the grid with a digit from 1 to 9. When the numbers in each row are added, you should arrive at the total in the right-hand column. When the numbers in each column are added, you should arrive at the total on the bottom line. The numbers in each diagonal must add up to the totals in the upper and lower right corners.

Party Dress

Magenta, Teal, and Hazel were invited to the same party, not knowing the others would also be there. When they arrived, they were wearing magenta, teal, and hazel dresses. The woman in the teal dress said, "Isn't it funny that our dress colors are the same as our names, but not 1 of us is wearing the dress that matches her name?" Magenta looked at the other 2 women and agreed. What color dress was each woman wearing?

Answers on page 182.

Rhyme Time: Test Rest

Answer each clue below with a pair of rhyming words. The numbers that follow each clue indicate how many letters are in each word. For example, "break during the exam" would be "test rest."

1. Break during the exam (4, 4): <u>TEST REST</u>

2. Seem to fly right off the shelves (4, 4): _____

3. Cheese store's giveaway (4, 4): _____

4. Part of a shoe store's inventory (4, 5): _____

5. Ankle-length South Pacific skirt (4, 6): _____

6. Reddish-faced pal (5, 5): _____

7. Specialized appliance repairperson (5, 5): _____

8. It put the buyer over her limit (5, 6): _____

9. Bag-carrier father (6, 5): _____

10. Tan compared to red (6, 5): _____

11. Barely noticeable chin feature (6, 6): _____

12. Didn't make a purchase (6, 6): _____

13. Auto accident (6, 6): _____

14. Reminder of a larger meteor (7, 6): _____

15. Perkier pet (7, 7): _____

Answers on page 182.

Square Grid

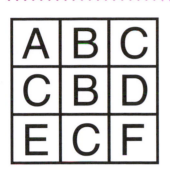

Each letter in the grid represents a digit from 1 to 9. Fill in the grid given that: (a) ABC and CBD are primes; (b) BBC and CDF are squares; and (c) ACE and ECF are cubes.

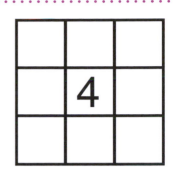

All Aboard

Find an expression to describe the picture below, and then rearrange the letters of this expression to form an 11-letter word. LLL, for example, is THREE L'S, whose rearranged letters form SHELTER.

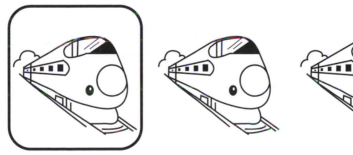

Answers on page 182.

Winter Wonders

Across

1. "It _____ a very good year"
4. Resistance units
8. Rich topsoil
12. Picnic pest
13. Gather, as grain
14. Otherwise
15. Fun winter "battle": 2 wds.
18. Mama's mate
19. Letter opener?
20. Sailor's assent
21. *Hee* _____
23. Gratuity
25. Chicken _____ king: 2 wds.
28. Service station purchase
30. Big faux pas
34. Athletes on the ice: 2 wds.
37. Durable alloy
38. Nevertheless

39. It's over an "i"
40. Precious stone
42. "..._____ the land of the free..."
44. Airport abbr.
47. Suds maker
49. Your mom's sister
53. In some houses, this is a winter tradition: 2 wds.
56. Agitate
57. Beginner
58. Fed. property overseer
59. River to the Caspian Sea
60. Auto pioneer Ransom Eli
61. Kind of curve

Down
1. Bee's cousin
2. "_____ and the King of Siam"
3. "Cut it out!"
4. Spherical body
5. Progress
6. Like about half of us
7. Water balloon sound
8. Oahu garland
9. Olympic gymnast Korbut
10. Pasty-faced
11. Parcel (out)
16. Baby's bawl
17. Warship
22. Eternal
24. Settle, as a debt
25. Contented sighs
26. Fate
27. Sharpshooter
29. Mata Hari, for 1

31. Provided with sustenance
32. To and _____
33. Winter hrs. in Boston
35. Beer barrel
36. Large, spotted cat
41. Phrase on a coat of arms
43. Pied Piper follower
44. Hosiery shade
45. Norse god of thunder
46. Diva's big song
48. _____ nitrate
50. Egg on
51. Loch of note
52. Afternoon socials
54. Under the weather
55. "Mayday!"

Answers on page 182.

ACCELERATE YOUR MENTAL POWERS

Wave of W's

ATTENTION   VISUAL SEARCH

There is a wave of things in this picture that begin with the letter "W." We count 14. How many can you find?

Answers on page 182.

Arrow Web

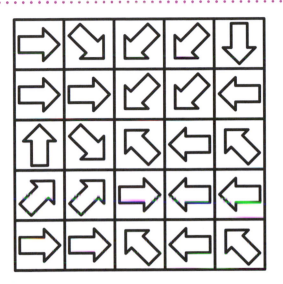

Blacken 8 arrows so that every arrow in the grid points to exactly 1 black arrow.

Logidoku in Shapes

The numbers 1 through 8 should appear once in every row, column, long diagonal, irregular shape (indicated by marked borders), and 2×4 grid (indicated by shaded or white blocks). With the help of the provided numbers in this square, can you complete the puzzle?

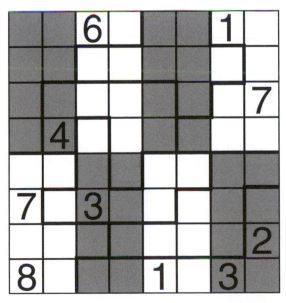

Answers on page 182.

Mirror—Camera

There's no trick here, only a challenge: Draw the mirror image of these familiar objects. You may find it harder than you think!

Give Sudoku a Shot

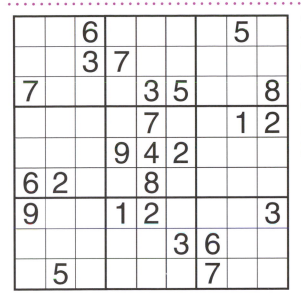

To solve a sudoku puzzle, place the numbers 1 through 9 only once in each row, column, and 3×3 box. Each puzzle has some numbers filled in—you just need to work out the rest. You'll never have to guess; each number can be found using the power of deduction.

Give Logidoku a Shot

The numbers 1 through 9 should appear once in every row, column, long diagonal, irregular shape (indicated by marked borders), and 3×3 grid (indicated by the shaded or white blocks). With the help of the provided numbers in this square, can you complete the puzzle?

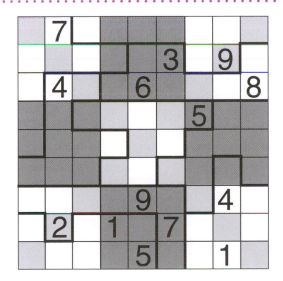

Answers on pages 182–183.

Accelerate Your Mental Powers

SUMsational!

1		4	3	1		6	5	**29**
2	3	1	4			5	8	**35**
4	2	6		2	7	8		**43**
2	3		7	6	1		4	**31**
1	6			5	7	8	5	**42**
3	5	3	8		4		2	**39**
		8	7	5	3		3	**34**
	8	7	5	9		4	1	**41**
18	**34**	**38**	**48**	**38**	**41**	**43**	**34**	**29**

35 (upper right corner total)

Fill each square in the grid with a digit from 1 to 9. When the numbers in each row are added, you should arrive at the total in the right-hand column. When the numbers in each column are added, you should arrive at the total on the bottom line. The numbers in each diagonal must add up to the totals in the upper and lower right corners.

Time Off

Change just 1 letter on each line to go from the top word to the bottom word. Each line will contain a new word. Do not change the order of the letters.

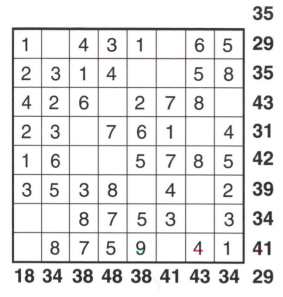

WORK

_____

_____

_____

_____

_____

PLAY

Answers on page 183.

110

May We Have a (Weird) Word With You?

These anagrams are a tad tricky, but there's a nice "aha!" moment when you get them.

Professor Leonardo Lingo, lover of linguistics, was holding forth in his freshman class, Weird Words 101. "Consider our language," he said. "It is exceedingly odd. Things don't seem to say what they mean. When we go to a football game, why do we yell, 'Go Bobcats!'? Why do they call the place where we *sit* the stands? How do we ever get off a nonstop flight? Since we sink into it slowly, what is so fast about quicksand?"

"But it's time for our pop quiz, which has no questions about soft drinks. Kindly anagram these phrases so they make sense, in a funny and paradoxical sort of way, in the context of the sentence."

1. Isn't it [SUE FLIRTS] _____ to eat your vegetables?

2. Is a [ROUTINE CAP] _____ something you take before a caution?

3. Isn't [DANK PIPING] _____ quite normal in kindergartens?

4. If a vegetarian eats vegetables, what does a [THAI RUMANIAN] _____ eat?

5. Why are there [NATTIER SETS] _____ in Hawaii?

Answers on page 183.

Fitting Words with a C

In this miniature crossword, the clues are listed randomly and are numbered only for convenience. Figure out the placement of the 9 answers. To help you out, 1 letter is inserted in the grid, and this is the *only* occurrence of that letter in the completed puzzle.

Clues
1. More than plump
2. Ancient Greek garment
3. China setting
4. Violin part
5. Touch on
6. Infidel
7. Cookware
8. T-bone
9. Trait carrier

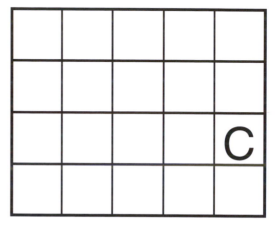

B-Dissection

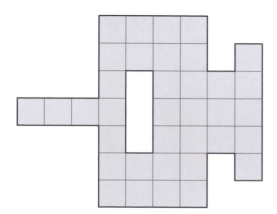

Using just your eyes, can you divide this larger shape into 4 smaller parts that are shaped the same? You can "cut" only along the lines of the grid. Shapes may be rotated or mirrored.

Answers on page 183.

Rhyme Time: Wind Kind

Answer each clue below with a pair of rhyming words. The numbers that follow each clue indicate how many letters are in each word. For example, "old-fashioned watch" would be "wind kind."

1. Old-fashioned watch (4, 4): <u>WIND KIND</u>

2. Concrete play area at school (4, 4): _____

3. South Florida college residence (4, 4): _____

4. Swindle on the tracks (4, 4): _____

5. Specialized utensil (4, 4): _____

6. Antique store purchase (4, 5): _____

7. A most impressive bird of prey (5, 5): _____

8. Molasses cookie (5, 5): _____

9. Clique within the cast (6, 5): _____

10. Favorite sixties flick (6, 5): _____

11. Temporary crown (6, 6): _____

12. Outdoor pest counter (7, 5): _____

Trivia on the Brain

The brain has "built-in backup systems" in some cases. If one pathway in the brain is damaged, there is often another pathway that will take over the function of the damaged one.

Answers on page 183.

Before and After

This 3-part puzzle is a fill-in-the-blank game, a word search, and a hidden message hunt. First, use the clues to find a word that completes the first word/phrase and begins the second. For example, the answer to Clue #1 would be "butterfly" because there's a monarch butterfly and a butterfly kiss. The number of blanks indicates the number of letters in each missing middle word. (Hint: The missing words are in alphabetical order.) As you go along, circle the missing words, which are all hidden in the butterfly-shape word-search grid. Words will run horizontally, vertically, or diagonally, but they will always be in a straight line. If you can't figure out a missing word from the clues, look for words in the grid.

Once you've circled all the words in the grid, read the uncircled letters in order from top to bottom to uncover a hidden message. The letters will be in order, but you'll need to break them into words and add punctuation as necessary. The hidden message is an appropriate observation about certain commercials you see on TV.

```
                S                               I
             T                          N
   N  N          I              E                    A  E
   L  O  L             C  P                    T  M  N
   H  I  O  Y  N       O  K          Y  S  P  E  G
   T  S  E  T  B  O  N  E  E  T  E  C  F  L
   O  I  R  I  B  U  T  T  E  R  F  L  Y  I
   E  V  Q  N  A  N  I  G  O  A  D  A  A  S
   F  I  G  U  R  E  N  R  N  P  D  M  F  H
      D  T  T  E  T  E  S  P  I  R  A  L
         R  H  S  N  L  S  E  H
      R  C  O  U  R  T  T  B  Q  A  S  D
   S  M  M  P  N  O  A  I  C  U  U  B  A  O
   D  A  Y  P  O  N  L  E  O  E  O  A  V  W
   S  S  T  O  C  K  I  N  G  N  F  D  S  E
   R  T  L  E  O     E  O        K  S  R  W  H
   O  E  R           S  R              E  E  A
   F  R                 T  E                 R  P
```

Clues

1.	MONARCH	_ _ _ _ _ _ _ _ _	KISS
2.	HAPPY AS A	_ _ _ _	CHOWDER
3.	LINCOLN	_ _ _ _ _ _ _ _ _ _	DRIFT
4.	TENNIS	_ _ _ _ _	JESTER
5.	WAY OFF IN THE	_ _ _ _ _ _ _	RUNNER
6.	LONG	_ _ _ _ _ _ _	OF LABOR
7.	BODY	_ _ _ _ _ _	JEOPARDY
8.	ROMAN	_ _ _ _ _ _	PENGUIN
9.	THE KING'S	_ _ _ _ _ _	MUFFIN
10.	GO	_ _ _ _ _	OF SPEECH
11.	FENCING	_ _ _ _ _	OF CEREMONIES
12.	U.S.	_ _ _ _	SESAME
13.	GOLDEN	_ _ _ _ _ _ _ _ _ _	KNOCKS
14.	SURPRISE	_ _ _ _ _	POOPER
15.	PICTURE	_ _ _ _ _ _	PITCH
16.	STRIP	_ _ _ _	FACE
17.	THAT'S A GOOD	_ _ _ _ _ _ _	MARK
18.	DOWNWARD	_ _ _ _ _	NOTEBOOK
19.	ACORN	_ _ _ _ _	RACQUET
20.	BUMPER	_ _ _ _ _ _	SHOCK
21.	NYLON	_ _ _ _ _ _ _	STUFFER
22.	I.Q.	_ _ _ _	TUBE
23.	DOUBTING	_ _ _ _ _ _	AQUINAS
24.	DENZEL	_ _ _ _ _ _ _ _ _	POST

Answers on page 183.

Time for Grooming

Before you groom, count the dots in this picture. But be sure what you count are dots!

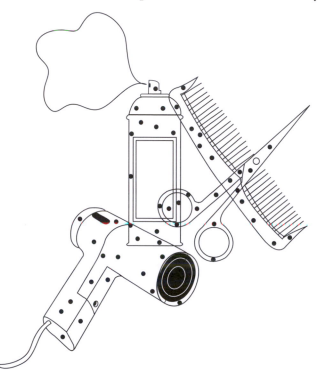

Counting Candy

COMPUTATION   LOGIC

Twins Andy and Randy share everything equally. On Halloween, Andy ran from house to house getting candy while Randy stopped to smell the flowers. At the end of the night, they compared the amount of candy in each bag. "We share everything equally," said Randy. "You have three times as many pieces of candy as I do." Andy was upset but handed over 20 pieces. "I said we share everything equally," said the flower-sniffing-and-candy-loving Randy. "Now you have twice as many pieces of candy as I do." In order for the twins to have equal amounts of candy, how many more pieces must Andy give to Randy? How many did each have at the start?

Answers on page 183.

Deal!

Every word listed below is contained within this group of letters. Words can be found horizontally, vertically, or diagonally. They may read either backward or forward.

```
E  R  H  C  U  E  T  W  Z  S  R  M  N  N
K  C  A  J  P  A  L  S  E  L  E  R  R  C
P  X  T  J  Q  W  C  D  W  C  K  M  T  J
I  D  K  Y  H  E  A  R  T  S  O  Q  S  T
N  A  L  M  L  P  S  R  I  J  P  T  N  K
O  E  C  M  S  B  P  D  Y  K  H  D  C  N
C  H  Z  U  M  D  I  T  G  G  U  A  B  O
H  S  K  R  B  Q  T  B  I  O  J  L  L  G
L  P  W  N  L  Y  R  E  T  K  F  D  A  C
E  E  L  I  V  I  Y  T  C  S  M  I  Y  K
R  E  K  G  D  Z  T  A  L  A  I  P  S  Q
L  H  N  G  A  K  L  Y  I  F  W  H  G  H
B  S  E  R  R  B  R  D  L  N  P  R  W  G
B  Q  C  S  O  L  I  T  A  I  R  E  T  Y
```

bridge	gin rummy	pinochle	spades
blackjack	go fish	poker	spit
crazy eights	hearts	sheepshead	war
euchre	kaluki	slapjack	whist
	old maid	solitaire	

Answers on page 183.

Instant Cure

Cryptograms are messages in substitution code. Break the code to read the message. For example, THE SMART CAT might become FVO QWGDF JGF if F is substituted for T, V for H, O for E, and so on.

XJOH D UAGT NF TAMUAY D

MABGTH'U VPPAYT VH AKOYVUDAH,

JO APPOYOT UA UABMJ-BK NF

R-YVFZ.   —JOHHF FABHCNVH

Think ABCD

Each row and column contains A, B, C, D, and 2 blank squares in random order. Each letter and number indicator refers to the first or second of the 4 letters encountered when traveling inward. Can you complete the grid?

Answers on page 184.

Sum Box

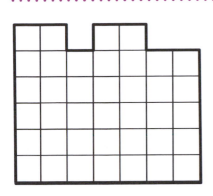

Place some digit figures into the grid, following the grid lines, so as to reach the maximum sum of digits possible. You can place the same digit more than once, and you can rotate the digits. But the digits cannot be reflected, nor can they overlap each other. What is the sum of the placed digits?

0123456789

Try Another Logidoku Challenge

LOGIC

The numbers 1 through 9 should appear once in every row, column, long diagonal, irregular shape (indicated by marked borders), and 3×3 grid (indicated by the shaded or white blocks). With the help of the provided numbers in this square, can you complete the puzzle?

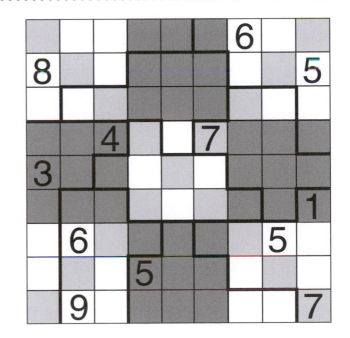

Answers on page 184.

Gram's Birthday

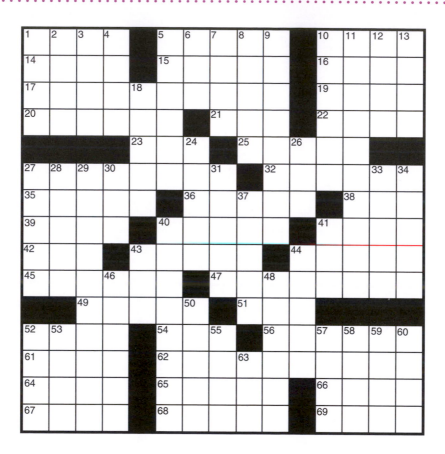

Across

1. It's dangerous when it flows
5. He wrote "Stars and Stripes Forever"
10. Like a senior citizen
14. Milton wrote them
15. Surrounding atmospheres
16. Sideless cart
17. Small units of weight
19. Unusual
20. Chant
21. Law: Fr.
22. Mean little kids
23. Branch of the serv.
25. Northeastern state of India
27. Enroll
32. Combination of high cards
35. The Southwest's Bret
36. Actress Debra
38. Reagan's son
39. Ages
40. Sprayed defensively

41. If it's "half," it's small
42. Where to get $$
43. Welfare allotments
44. Civil War general
45. Oklahoman
47. Kitchen utensil
49. Showers with stones
51. Eternally: poet.
52. Sounds of laughter: 2 wds.
54. Once _____ blue moon: 2 wds.
56. Things to eat
61. Smell
62. Heart examination
64. Eat
65. Silkworms
66. Tear down, in England
67. Engl. monetary term
68. Coarse grass
69. Tennis stadium honoree

Down

1. Places
2. It's between Yemen and Oman
3. Escape port for air
4. Regarding: 2 wds.
5. Wisest
6. Belonging to us
7. Russia's _____ Mountains
8. Where Robert Louis Stevenson died
9. Helped
10. Name of 6 popes
11. Parser
12. Wyatt _____
13. Colors

18. Sign on a lab door: 2 wds.
24. Himalayan kingdom
26. Part of a tennis match
27. Flightless S.A. birds
28. "Keep an _____ the ground": 2 wds.
29. Record player
30. Possessive pronoun
31. "Camptown _____"
33. Spanish earl
34. "Abandon hope, all ye who _____ here" (Dante)
37. *Beau* _____
40. Tenons's companions: var.
41. Charlottetown is its cap.
43. Singer Shannon
44. Driver Andretti
46. Closer
48. Edit
50. Trap
52. Devices for carrying bricks
53. Mine entrance
55. Sere
57. Taj Mahal city
58. Depression and gun orgs.
59. Elan
60. Duck
63. Hammarskjöld of the U.N.

Answers on page 184.

Accelerate Your Mental Powers

The Answer Man, Part 1

VERBAL
MEMORY

Read the following story. Then see if you can correctly answer questions about what you've read.

Invictus Sigafoos was writing a book. Not just any book, mind you. This was *The Book of Answers*. It would be a guaranteed bestseller, he assured his friends, because it would have all the answers. "Got a question?" he said to his pal Eddie Shrdlu. "The answer is in the book."

"Come on, Vic," said Eddie. "Any question?"

"You got it, pal. Go ahead, ask a question."

"Okay. What can go up a chimney down but not down a chimney up?"

"That's on page 3," said Vic. "An umbrella."

"All right," said Eddie. "Pretty good. Here's another one: What is the one 11-letter word that all Harvard graduates spell incorrectly?"

"Page 17," said Vic. " 'Incorrectly.' "

"I'm impressed!" said Eddie. "So if you know everything, tell me this: What is the meaning of life?"

"Everyone knows that," said Vic. "42."

"Page 42?"

"No, just 42. Didn't you read *The Hitchhiker's Guide to the Galaxy*?"

The book was published and became a bestseller, just as Invictus had predicted. On his book tour, he arrived in Milwaukee and went to the hotel he was supposed to be staying at—only to find there wasn't a room to be had. The place was sold out!

"But I have a reservation!" said Invictus.

122

"I'm sorry, sir," said the desk clerk. "Some people have extended their stays. We don't have a single room."

Invictus needed an answer, but this one wasn't in his book. He had to think fast. He was the Answer Man!

"So," he said to the desk clerk. "If the President of the United States was in town and needed a place to stay, are you telling me you wouldn't get him a room?"

"Well," said the desk clerk. "If it was the President, I'm sure we would find him a room somehow."

"Great!" said Invictus. "I'll take his room! He's not coming."

The Answer Man, Part II

(Don't read this until you've read the previous page!)

1. What was the name of the President of the United States in 1981? (This is a trick question!)

2. What was the name of Eddie's book?

3. What city is named as being on the book tour?

4. What is the meaning of life?

Easy to Do

LANGUAGE

Read the following phrase.

C(AKE)

Answers on page 184.

Crisscross Puzzle

Place the words below into this crossword.

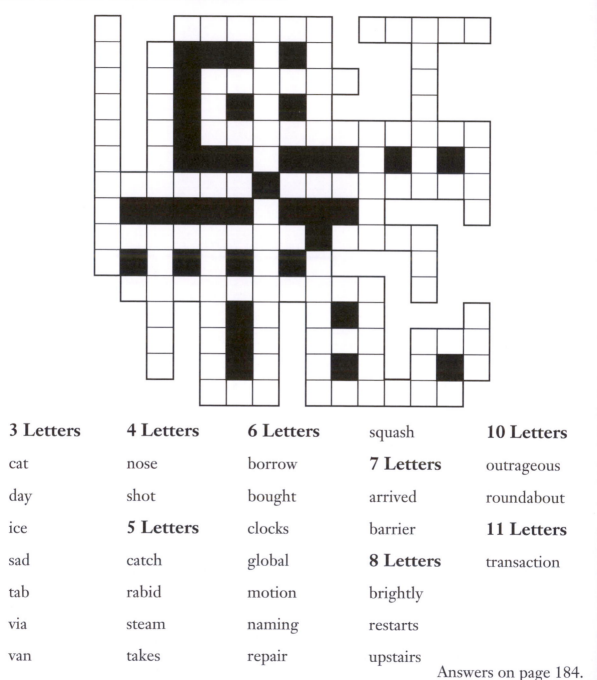

3 Letters	4 Letters	6 Letters	squash	10 Letters
cat	nose	borrow	7 Letters	outrageous
day	shot	bought	arrived	roundabout
ice	5 Letters	clocks	barrier	11 Letters
sad	catch	global	8 Letters	transaction
tab	rabid	motion	brightly	
via	steam	naming	restarts	
van	takes	repair	upstairs	

Answers on page 184.

Move the Matchsticks

PLANNING **SPATIAL REASONING**

The button in the equation below stands for the multiplication sign. Obviously, V multiplied by V is not II. Move 2 matchsticks to new positions to make the equation correct. The button must still be considered as the multiplication sign, and the final equation must retain the equal sign. No damaging of matchsticks is allowed. The overlapping of matchsticks is allowed.

Tennis Aces

CREATIVE THINKING **LANGUAGE**

Roddick is playing Federer in the Wimbledon final. Roddick serves aces on 6 consecutive points, during which time Federer does not touch the ball. However, Roddick is still losing the match. What is the precise score in the match?

Trivia on the Brain

Your hypothalamus plays a vital role in keeping conditions inside your body constant. It does this by regulating your thirst, hunger, and body temperature, among other things.

Answers on page 184.

Rhyme Time: Top Crop

Answer each clue below with a pair of rhyming words. The numbers that follow each clue indicate how many letters are in each word. For example, "farmer's pride" would be "top crop."

1. Farmer's pride (3, 4): __TOP CROP__

2. Chicken server's suggestion (3, 5): _____

3. Corncob, e.g. (4, 4): _____

4. It makes swimmers shiver (4, 4): _____

5. Temporary sales outlet (4, 5): _____

6. Golfer's need, descriptively (5, 4): _____

7. Dead letter office contents (5, 4): _____

8. Hoard money (5, 4): _____

9. Slight blemish (5, 5): _____

10. Timepiece inventory (5, 5): _____

11. It's not a real jail (5, 5): _____

12. Military man in his first battle (5, 6): _____

13. Traveling without baggage (5, 6): _____

14. Race track (5, 6): _____

15. He finds game faster (6, 6): _____

Answers on page 184.

ABCD with a C

Every cell in the 6×6 grid contains 1 of the following 4 letters: A, B, C, or D. No letter can be horizontally or vertically adjacent to itself. The tables above and to the left of the grid indicate how many times each letter appears in that column or row. Can you complete the grid? We have placed one C in the grid to get you going.

	A	3	0	0	2	2	2
	B	0	3	2	1	2	1
	C	1	3	2	1	1	1
A B C D	D	2	0	2	2	1	2

A	B	C	D						
2	2	1	1						
1	1	2	2						
3	2	0	1						
1	1	1	3						
0	3	3	0						
2	0	2	2				C		

A Sudoku Enigma

To solve a sudoku puzzle, place the numbers 1 through 9 only once in each row, column, and 3×3 box. Each puzzle has some numbers filled in—you just need to work out the rest. You'll never have to guess; each number can be found using the power of deduction.

	4			1			5	
					6			9
9	1		3					
		9				5		
7	6			2			3	8
		1				7		
					8		6	2
6			1					
	3			4			8	

Answers on page 185.

Nation of N's

Within this picture is a nation of things beginning with the letter "N." We count 12 things. How many can you find?

Trivia on the Brain

By age 5, the brain has gained almost its full weight.

Answers on page 185.

Word Columns

To find the statement, put the letters that appear in the bottom half of the puzzle into the column of boxes above them. The letters may not be listed in the exact order in which they appear in the boxes. Mark off used letters at the bottom. A letter may be used only once. The black boxes represent the space between words.

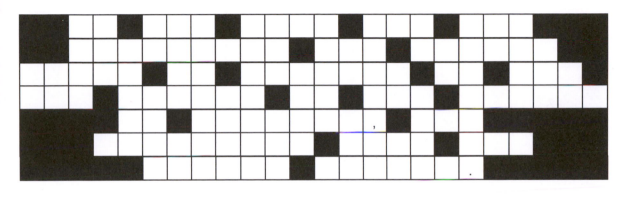

```
              e   a
          o   w   e       l   y   t       w   r   w
          o   o   c   k   i   m   g   a   K   n   a   i   c   N   s
      N   l   t   S   t   C   u   m   n   o   f   D   i   r   o   t   a   n   l
      e   t   l   a   r   c   r   k   e   l   r   h   e   d   h   i   s   y   m   b
  t   h   a   o   f   g   n   n   e   s   u   y   w   s   e   h   k   h   t   t   d   e   s
  u   n   t   i   e   f   e   o   d   n   r   e   u   n   S   g   t   a   e   a   w   a   a   s
```

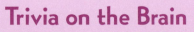

Trivia on the Brain

The B vitamins are very important for top mental function, as are the lycopene found in tomatoes, vitamin K found in broccoli, and antioxidants found in blueberries.

Answer on page 185.

Count Me In!

COMPUTATION   **LOGIC**

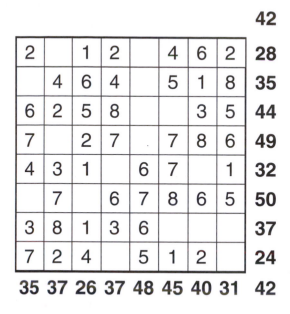

								42
2		1	2		4	6	2	28
	4	6	4		5	1	8	35
6	2	5	8			3	5	44
7		2	7		7	8	6	49
4	3	1		6	7		1	32
	7		6	7	8	6	5	50
3	8	1	3	6				37
7	2	4		5	1	2		24
35	**37**	**26**	**37**	**48**	**45**	**40**	**31**	**42**

Fill each square in the grid with a digit from 1 to 9. When the numbers in each row are added, you should arrive at the total in the right-hand column. When the numbers in each column are added, you should arrive at the total on the bottom line. The numbers in each diagonal must add up to the totals in the upper and lower right corners.

Rectangles in Mass

ATTENTION   **VISUAL SEARCH**

Do you know what a rectangle is? How many are in this drawing?

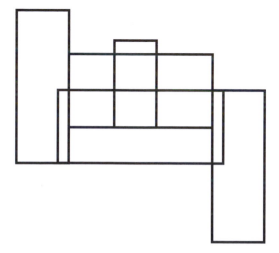

Answers on page 185.

Geometric Shapes

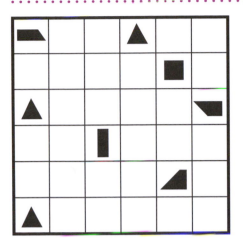

Divide the whole grid into smaller geometric shapes by drawing straight lines either following the grid lines or the full diagonals of the square cells. Each formed shape must contain only 1 symbol, which represents that shape. A rectangle symbol cannot be contained in a square. A trapezoid has 2 parallel sides and 2 nonparallel sides.

Three for Two

GENERAL KNOWLEDGE   LANGUAGE

That is, 3 letters for 2 answers!

Here's how it works: We provide 3 letters and a category, and you come up with 2 answers from that category in which the 3 letters appear in the same sequence. Example: If the category is SIGNS OF THE ZODIAC, and we gave you the 3 letters COR, your answers would be S<u>COR</u>PIO and CAPRI<u>COR</u>N. Or if we had given you the letters ARI in the same category, you could have chosen 2 signs from AQU<u>ARI</u>US, SAGITT<u>ARI</u>US or <u>ARI</u>ES.

Letters	Category	
1. Car	Food	_____
2. Eri	Great Lakes	_____
3. Mbe	Months	_____
4. Har	Deserts	_____
5. Gar	European countries	_____

Answers on page 185.

M Is for Mystery

An anagram is a word or phrase made up of the rearranged letters of another word or phrase. Fill in the blanks in the conversation below by solving each anagram.

Merely Neat, and Tom Sawyer—or, translated from the anagram, "Elementary, My Dear Watson!"

The great detective Shellshock Rome had settled himself into a comfortable leather armchair in Raffles, his gentlemen's club. Across from him, on the other side of a chessboard, sat his loyal companion, Two-Star Condo. Rome puffed slowly on his calabash, his slender fingers cradling the polished meerschaum bowl that looked like carved ivory but was, in fact, fashioned from a hard white clay. Condo, with white, moved pawn to e4. Rome smiled, knowing that his old friend could rarely resist the Ruy Lopez, a popular Spanish opening in chess.

"Cultural literacy is in decline, Condo," said Rome. "Hardly any of this generation has seen MAN OF STEEL CHALET _____ —Bogart, Lorre, Greenstreet!—much less read the book. I suppose HAG AT CHARITIES _____ _____ is the most successful female mystery author, since she has been outsold only by the Bible and Shakespeare! I rather enjoy her pleasant mysteries featuring OUR HELICOPTER _____, though those British cozies with SIMPLE ARMS _____ never quite caught my fancy. I do like Dorothy Sayers's creation, MY SPIDERWORT EEL _____, a scholar and a gentleman."

"What about GUINEA DUSTUP _____, Rome?" asked Condo. "Surely you can't dismiss GLAD AEROPLANE _____!" As expected, Condo's second move was king's knight to f3.

"I'd just as soon watch CHILEAN ARCH _____," sniffed Rome.

Answers on page 185.

Another Fitting Words with a G

LOGIC

LANGUAGE PLANNING

In this miniature crossword, the clues are listed randomly and are numbered only for convenience. Figure out the placement of the 9 answers. To help you out, 1 letter is inserted in the grid, and this is the *only* occurrence of that letter in the completed puzzle.

Clues
1. Ape
2. Turn away
3. Nefarious
4. Engrave with acid
5. Leafy "fence"
6. Comedians
7. Floor model
8. Deadly sin
9. Fortitude

On the Right Track

LANGUAGE PLANNING

Change just 1 letter on each line to go from the top word to the bottom word. Each line will contain a new word. Do not change the order of the letters.

PLANE

_____

_____ a braid

_____

_____ an inflammation

_____

TRAIN

Answers on page 185.

Cole Porter Songs

American composer Cole Porter wrote some of the most memorable tunes of the early 20th century. The titles of many of his hit and not-as-well-known songs are listed below and found in this grid. Circle all of them.

Anything Goes

Begin the Beguine

Brush Up Your Shakespeare

C'est Magnifique

Cherry Pies Ought to Be You

Don't Fence Me In

Down in the Depths

Friendship

From This Moment On

Get Out of Town

I Get a Kick Out of You

I Love Paris

Always True to You in My Fashion

It's De-Lovely

I've Got My Eyes on You

Let's Do It

Night and Day

Ridin' High

We Open in Venice

Well Did You Evah?

Why Shouldn't I?

You'd Be So Easy to Love

You're Sensational

You're the Top

```
N N B Y T O F R I E E W H N I G E Y W L B R U S H U P Y
H O T O H I O L E T T N D G A Y I O E L E T S D O S O R
Y U I U B F O V A N Y P M N I W G U O O I C B E G U N B
O N E H B R O D R S O D Y I E H E D P D T H L A R N R I
U L E T S O U C S T T T O O E F N B E O S E N E T U I I
D E I M G A S O E T H O P W T R M I N N I P S N S E B E
B H V I G E F H Y I E E C A N I R U D T E E G H E U R C
E F Y O E O T Y N E N L T E E I O A S I N D U I O D U E
S R B F L E N G M I B F R O S Y N D E S R P I Y L O S S
O I E I R O G V N N T O U Y F T E T A B Y M N F W N H T
Y E G U N O T V T G I H T O A L M T H O S O Y R T T U M
I B O G E S E Y A E I U T T O O I A U E S N O O N F P A
F Y B S D N I E S T N U O V H O I R G E D S U M I E I E
R I L O I O D O W A O O E Y N G S D Y N I E R I G N N W
I C O C L B N S H K E L T A O H U E T Y I G P S H I Y E
E H E I T S D T C A Y O L N A T Y O S F E F N T U E W O
N E B R U S I I F G V U S K E M E D S T N I I G H H D L
D P D O N S K L O E S E E E T M O U O E G O E Q Y S O W
S L I E R A R G O O N S U O B W O U R H I B L S U E N E
H E G H T C D O N V P C G O U D T M T T E P H L O E T L
A T I E S I T S D E E E E Y O U A S H S O Y V W S F L
N H G N L D G I A E V P P M F D N O T I U Y E R E U E D
Y I C E S T N R Y I L H A T E D I N Y L H I A R R H N I
T U R I O T E E N D E D O R D I I D D S L T N W D E I D
H N Y O U D B B I H T W N A I G N N L I L O M A L E H Y
I Y O U D B E T Y R N L Y I E S T S I L C H E O S A T C
N N I G W E O P E N F D H B P I M L E T E D O N R O M V
Y O U B R U S H U P Y W F R I E N D S L E W T T S F A I
```

Answers on page 186.

Crypto-Animal Families

Cryptograms are messages in substitution code. Break the code to read the message. For example, THE SMART CAT might become FVO QWGDF JGF if F is substituted for T, V for H, O for E, and so on.

Each Crypto-Family is a list of related words in code. Each family has its own code.

1. On the Farm	2. At the Zoo	3. In the Ocean
AMBANHD	EFAAGAGHIDJK	FLEPC
CEFK	LEFMG	ICEP
AEJ	HFPNL	AGBAPC
MEGIH	PFLIBBN	IAHKDBEJ
CEEIH	NONAEIMH	RMPNLHK
OPANRBDC	PGLFOOI	PMSIACB
IMHHS	RNCLI	MJIACB
IJBDH	SIMPILGG	IAEBTHIL
GFTTBK	KMISNK	UCPPJTHIL
MEPDO	OFGM	ILEBV

Answers on page 186.

Psychics for Hire

A hundred people showed up to be interviewed by a brokerage company looking to hire psychics. Stock certificates from 5 different blue-chip companies were placed in a 5-drawer filing cabinet, 1 in each drawer. The psychics were asked to predict which stock was in which drawer. In order to meet new government hiring regulations, the company would only be hiring psychics who correctly predicted the contents in 4 out of the 5 drawers. After the psychics made their predictions and the drawers were opened, the company found that 7 psychics got none of the drawers right, 13 got only 1 drawer right, 22 got only 2 drawers right, and 39 got only 3 drawers right. How many psychics did the brokerage company hire?

A Capital Puzzle!

ATTENTION · VISUAL SEARCH

Some important places are lurking in these sentences. Can you figure out what they are?

1. "Here's the plan: Sing along with the karaoke and try not to embarrass yourself!"

2. Radioactive isotope? Ka-boom!

3. "Oh yes," said the florist, "I know that garden very well."

4. You can get good deals on the wholesale market.

5. Architect: "Send those gazebos to Newark."

Answers on page 186.

A Logidoku Enigma

LOGIC

The numbers 1 through 9 should appear once in every row, column, long diagonal, irregular shape (indicated by marked borders), and 3×3 grid (indicated by shaded or white blocks). With the help of the provided numbers in this square, can you complete the puzzle?

Adding Is Fun

COMPUTATION   LOGIC

Fill each square in the grid with a digit from 1 to 9. When the numbers in each row are added, you should arrive at the total in the right-hand column. When the numbers in each column are added, you should arrive at the total on the bottom line. The numbers in each diagonal must add up to the totals in the upper and lower right corners.

						21
	3		8	6	4	**28**
4	7	1		3	5	**29**
6	4		5		7	**31**
9		2	8	2		**34**
	6	1	5	3		**18**
1			4	7	9	**32**
23	**28**	**20**	**39**	**28**	**34**	**30**

Answers on page 186.

MASTER YOUR INTELLECT

Lots of Dots in Gardening

Summer has come, and it's time to plant and water your rosebush, but first, count the dots in this picture. It's harder than you think.

Don't Answer

Read the following phrase.

BEthebushAT

Answers on page 186.

Europe Is Calling Me!

Every listed country is contained within this group of letters. Names can be found horizontally, vertically, or diagonally. They may read either backward or forward.

Y	T	N	A	F	L	C	M	D	D	I	C	V	Y	L	Y
C	M	O	I	C	G	L	E	P	R	N	Y	R	M	R	N
T	V	R	S	T	Q	N	M	E	E	P	A	H	P	Y	D
C	R	W	S	K	M	M	L	N	C	G	O	L	Q	C	R
I	X	A	U	A	Q	A	H	T	N	M	P	L	N	T	M
L	L	Y	R	S	N	M	F	U	A	L	J	Q	A	I	V
B	M	K	V	D	W	K	H	P	R	Q	F	T	C	N	F
U	A	U	S	T	R	I	A	R	F	R	P	X	P	K	D
P	T	N	N	F	W	N	T	N	Y	N	A	M	R	E	G
E	U	K	P	E	F	K	D	Z	R	L	M	G	Y	T	N
R	R	T	X	F	C	J	N	K	E	D	F	L	R	I	P
H	K	X	K	P	Y	E	Z	C	T	R	A	R	A	N	G
C	E	W	W	R	D	V	E	L	T	T	L	P	R	J	K
E	Y	L	P	X	H	K	C	R	I	N	S	A	L	P	K
Z	H	E	N	G	L	A	N	D	G	T	M	W	N	Y	R
C	L	A	G	U	T	R	O	P	R	L	J	L	R	D	G

Austria	Germany	Poland
Czech Republic	Greece	Portugal
Denmark	Hungary	Russia
England	Ireland	Spain
Finland	Italy	Switzerland
France	Norway	Turkey

Answers on page 186.

Lottery Logic

Gary, Hurley, and Joe pool their money every week to play the lottery. Gary puts in $3, Hurley puts in $2, Joe puts in $1. With this money, they buy 6 tickets. Because they put in different amounts and because Joe doesn't appear to be too bright, they decide to divide any winnings the following way: Gary would get one half, Hurley would get one third, and Joe would get one ninth. The friends finally got a winner, and the prize was $34. The prize was paid out in dollar bills, and none of them had any coins to make change. Gary and Hurley couldn't figure out how to divide the dollar bills in the pot. Joe reached into his pocket, pulled something out, and the friends were able to divide their winnings according to the agreed-upon deal. What did Joe pull out of his pocket?

Drop Me a Line

Change just 1 letter on each line to go from the top word to the bottom word. Each line will contain a new word. Do not change the order of the letters.

FISH

———

———

———

———

———

HOOK

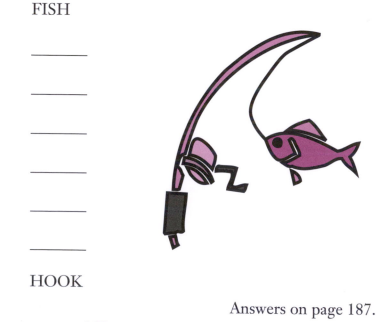

Answers on page 187.

Throng of T's

Inside this picture is a throng of things beginning with the letter "T." We count 17. How many can you find?

Trivia on the Brain

Both the brain and the computer need energy. The brain needs nutrients like oxygen and sugar for power; the computer needs electricity to function.

Answers on page 187.

A Super Logidoku Challenge

The numbers 1 through 9 should appear once in every row, column, long diagonal, irregular shape (indicated by marked borders), and 3×3 box (indicated by shaded or white blocks). With the help of the provided numbers in this square, can you complete the puzzle?

Famed Fabulist

LANGUAGE   LOGIC

Cryptograms are messages in substitution code. Break the code to read the message. For example, THE SMART CAT might become FVO QWGDF JGF if F is substituted for T, V for H, O for E, and so on.

PCSO GLU KLO, QM PDLBSPSIU, L OALEN KCI ASENB SU

GSB-OSFPC HNUPJDM Q. H. LUHSNUP RDNNHN. CSO OPIDSNO

LDN OPSAA PLJRCP LO GIDLA ANOOIUO. OIGN IT CSO GIOP

TLGSASLD OPIDSNO LDN "PCN PIDPISON LUB PCN CLDN" LUB

"PCN QIM KCI HDSNB KIAT." CN SO VUIKU LO LNOIW.

Answers on page 187.

A Digitized Crossword

COMPUTATION LOGIC

Use the clues to determine which of the digits 1 through 9 belongs in each square. No zeros are used.

Across

1. A prime number
3. A prime number
5. Consecutive digits, ascending
7. Its last digit is the sum of its first 2 digits
8. Consecutive digits, descending
10. Reversal of 3–Across
11. Eight more than 3–Across

Down

1. A power of 2 (i.e., a number in the doubling sequence 2, 4, 8, 16 …)
2. In this 5-digit number ABCDE, the 2-digit number AB times C equals the 2-digit number DE
3. A palindrome
4. A composite (non-prime) number
6. Consecutive digits, ascending
8. A multiple of 3
9. A multiple of 7

Equalizing Heads

CREATIVE THINKING LANGUAGE

There are 23 ordinary coins lying flat on a table in a completely dark room. Besides the 15 that have heads up, 8 have tails up. You are in the room and must separate the coins into 2 groups, each of which has the same number of heads up. You may turn over coins but you cannot distinguish heads from tails in any way. No tricks are involved here.

Answers on page 187.

Tourist Attraction

Find an anagram for each of the words below. The anagrams will answer the following clues. Write the correct anagram on the line by each clue. When completed correctly, the first letters of the anagrams will spell the name of a tourist attraction.

ROVED	TRANCE	DOWRY	HENRI
NITER	ENEMY	TOILER	LACED
BELOW	REIGNS	VOILE	

Clues

1. English seaport _____
2. Dormant _____
3. Sinatra, e.g. _____
4. Bee's drink _____
5. Macaroni shape _____
6. Arab country _____
7. Talkative _____
8. Shade of green _____
9. European river _____
10. Hang around _____
11. Decorative sticker _____

Answers on page 187.

146

Word Columns

To find the statement, put the letters that appear in the bottom half of the puzzle into the column of boxes above them. The letters may not be listed in the exact order in which they appear in the statement. Mark off used letters at the bottom. A letter may be used only once. The black boxes represent the space between words.

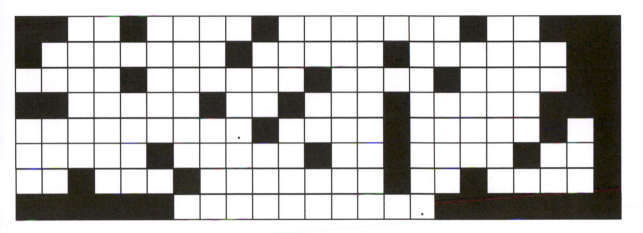

```
                                        s   i

        y           i   r           i       g   t       t           p

    a   n       w   n   f   h   m   L   a   t   o       n   i       d   t

  l   u   d   t   l   s   g   a   f   i   t   s   d       l   i   b   n   i

i   i   d   i   n   i   t   k   r   t   d   h   s   e       f   s   o   o   t   e

s   p   s   e   w   d   l   g   o   t   s   o   e   o   w   m   y   n   t   l   o   n

y   a   M   t   d   a   i   t   e   e   h   n   d   o   s   l   a   g   h   t   n   a

p   t   r   a   e   e   f   l   i   a   s   n   h   e   s   n   r   t   o   n   h   k
```

Answer on page 187.

Sudoku on the Brain

To solve a sudoku puzzle, place the numbers 1 through 9 only once in each row, column, and 3×3 box. Each puzzle has some numbers filled in—you just need to work out the rest. You'll never have to guess; each number can be found using the power of deduction.

Try an Odd-Even Logidoku

The numbers 1 through 9 should appear once in every row, column, long diagonal, irregular shape (indicated by marked borders), and 3×3 box (indicated by shaded and white blocks). With the help of the provided numbers in this square and the even-number indicators (E), can you complete the puzzle?

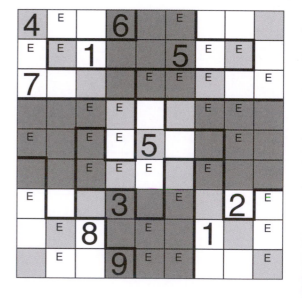

Answers on page 187.

Math—The Final Frontier

Fill each square in the grid with a digit from 1 to 9. When the numbers in each row are added, you should arrive at the total in the right-hand column. When the numbers in each column are added, you should arrive at the total on the bottom line. The numbers in each diagonal must add up to the totals in the upper and lower right corners.

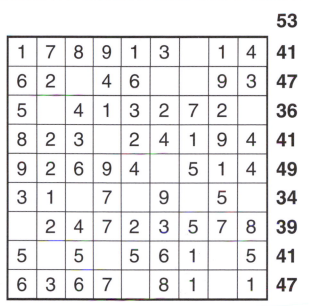

53

1	7	8	9	1	3		1	4	**41**
6	2		4	6			9	3	**47**
5		4	1	3	2	7	2		**36**
8	2	3		2	4	1	9	4	**41**
9	2	6	9	4		5	1	4	**49**
3	1		7		9		5		**34**
	2	4	7	2	3	5	7	8	**39**
5		5		5	6	1		5	**41**
6	3	6	7		8	1		1	**47**

44 34 46 56 33 52 31 42 37   36

Rating the Guys

According to the dating service's new rating system, Buddy and Freddy are 6's. Bob and Ned are 3's. Jonathan is a 9. What is Antonio?

Answers on pages 187–188.

Angry Prosecutor

Find a place in the grid for each of the words listed.

3 Letters

ale

asp

den

ion

PXs

rep

see

4 Letters

act I

Agee

aloe

army

cabs

claw

dope

ERNO

Inez

kite

Leah

peep

rara

rasp

rely

Saul

seed

tied

5 Letters

acrid

Anton

crone

impel

leave

necks

Perez

Russo

saber

scare

shyer

titan

6 Letters

Assisi

Lenten

mops up

sepsis

smiths

stir up

7 Letters

aerator

Bambino

classic

critter

elevate

eyesore

Natalie

renewed

8 Letters

elegance

in a sense

polestar

Roth IRAs

13 Letters

cross-examiner

Answers on page 188.

Mirror—Briefcase

Draw the mirror image of these objects. You will find this task quite challenging!

Rhyme Time: Why Try

Answer each clue below with a pair of rhyming words. The numbers that follow each clue indicate how many letters are in each word. For example, "underachiever's credo" would be "why try."

1. Underachiever's credo (3, 3): <u>WHY TRY</u>

2. Culinary mariners (4, 4): _____

3. She can afford the best of brooms (4, 5): _____

4. Attorney's illegal billing (4, 5): _____

5. Aid for river-crossers (4, 5): _____

6. Great ringer (5, 4): _____

7. Time protector (5, 4): _____

8. A.M. gatherers at restaurant (6, 5): _____

9. Revolutionary new pedal (6, 5): _____

10. Require the study of poetry (6, 5): _____

11. How to close the mouth of a dog? (6, 6): _____

12. Where to find roots (7, 5): _____

13. Underachiever's credo (5, 8): _____

14. In search of comic relief (5, 8): _____

15. Monotonous tiles (6, 8): _____

Answers on page 188.

Dan Shocker!

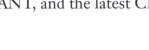
LANGUAGE

An anagram is a word made up of the rearranged letters of another word (as in *made* and *dame*). *Dan Shocker* is an oddly apt anagram for *anchor desk*. Make sense of the following sentences by solving these anagrams.

"We have SNEAKING BREW tonight, folks," said the NEW ACTRESS.

"We have a BANDED CACTI on TOYS R US—EXT XII. Let's go to our HEROIC PELT, CHIPPER SOX, followed by a FIRED-UP FAT CAT."

Later, there were stories on a GROUCHIER ANT, and the latest CREOLE GAVE NOTICE.

"How'd it go, boss?" the ART-DECO BRAS asked the CURED PRO, after the show.

"Well, you're no IRATE TOWN CLERK," came the answer. "You left out that little detail called the SEA-OTTER FURY. Aside from that, it was just swell."

Know Your Numbers

COMPUTATION   LOGIC

Use the clues to determine which of the numbers 1 through 9 belongs in each square. No zeros are used.

Hint: There is 1 set of numbers that will intersect to make 3–Across and 2–Down work.

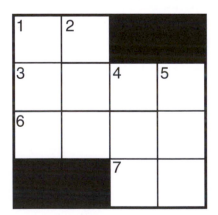

Across
1. A multiple of 13
3. The sum of its digits is 5
6. A multiple of 9
7. A prime number

Down
1. Its last digit is the sum of its first 2 digits
2. The sum of its digits is 20
4. A multiple of 17
5. A perfect square

Answers on page 188.

Find the Shape

In the grid, find a stylized shape *exactly* as that shown next to the grid. The shape can be rotated but not mirrored.

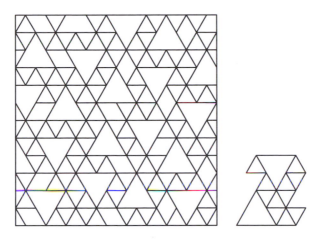

Fitting Words with a P

In this miniature crossword, the clues are listed randomly and are numbered only for convenience. Figure out the placement of the 9 answers. To help you out, 1 letter is inserted in the grid, and this is the *only* occurrence of that letter in the completed puzzle.

Clues

1. Restaurant posting
2. Hair salon items
3. Craze
4. Summer _____
5. Plunge a knife into
6. Perpendicular
7. Fend off
8. Egg-shape
9. Top of cup

Answers on page 188.

Push for the Pinnacle

COMPUTATION   **LOGIC**

Help the mountaineer reach the summit by filling in all of the numbers in these boulder circles. Each boulder is the sum of the numbers in the boulders that immediately support it. For example: 2 + 3 = 5. If a total is 10 or more, just write in the second digit. For example: 7 + 6 = 13; write in 3.

Horrific Riders

ANALYSIS   **CREATIVE THINKING**

What is the next letter of biblical significance?

P W F __

Answers on page 188.

The Final Sudoku Challenge

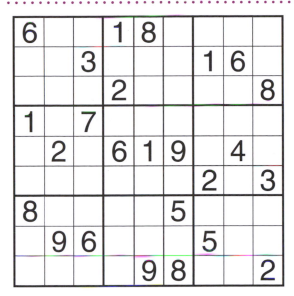

To solve a sudoku puzzle, place the numbers 1 through 9 only once in each row, column, and 3×3 box. Each puzzle has some numbers filled in—you just need to work out the rest. You'll never have to guess; each number can be found using the power of deduction.

The Final Logidoku Challenge

The numbers 1 through 9 should appear once in every row, column, long diagonal, irregular shape (indicated by marked borders), and 3×3 box (indicated by shaded or white blocks). With the help of the provided numbers in this square, can you complete the puzzle?

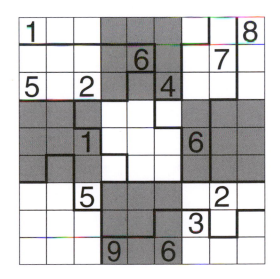

Answers on pages 188–189.

Potpourri of P's

There is a potpourri of things in this picture beginning with the letter "P." We count 17. How many can you find?

Trivia on the Brain

Why does your brain feel tired when you think a lot? Your brain consumes a lot of energy—as much as one-fifth of all the energy you get from food. Brain scans show that thinking uses up a lot of energy (as revealed by increased blood flow).

Answers on page 189.

Touchdown!

Every team listed below is contained within this group of letters. Names can be found horizontally, vertically, or diagonally. They may read either backward or forward.

```
Z  R  J  F  X  F  S  N  I  K  S  D  E  R  F
N  N  P  S  N  O  C  L  A  F  R  M  J  S  O
B  P  R  B  G  Q  J  E  T  S  B  M  Y  R  R
T  N  A  B  E  A  R  S  J  H  Q  O  D  E  T
V  E  Y  T  R  N  P  S  H  T  B  G  V  D  Y
T  H  X  R  L  G  Q  M  W  K  R  S  I  N
P  L  S  A  J  I  D  A  O  A  S  R  N  A  I
A  X  T  V  N  L  O  C  L  T  R  T  I  R  N
N  R  N  E  M  S  S  T  E  S  S  Q  H  K  E
T  J  A  N  H  A  D  E  S  F  L  V  P  Q  R
H  Z  I  S  I  X  L  N  E  S  M  N  L  B  S
E  R  G  N  B  E  W  I  L  T  N  L  O  P  M
R  Q  T  D  R  O  H  K  Z  K  K  O  D  N  P
S  S  H  S  R  C  B  D  C  V  Q  D  I  R  V
L  T  R  B  S  E  A  H  A  W  K  S  R  L  H
```

Bears	**Falcons**	**Panthers**	**Redskins**
Bengals	**Forty-Niners**	**Patriots**	**Saints**
Browns	**Giants**	**Raiders**	**Seahawks**
Chiefs	**Jets**	**Rams**	**Steelers**
Cowboys	**Lions**	**Ravens**	**Texans**
Dolphins			

Answers on page 189.

All the World's a Stage

Change DRAMA to STAGE in 8 steps. Change just 1 letter on each line to go from the top word to the bottom word. Each line will contain a new word. Do not change the order of the letters.

DRAMA

_____

_____

_____

_____

_____

_____

_____

STAGE

A Shapely Challenge

How many quadrilateral shapes—shapes with 4 sides—are in this mind-boggling puzzle?

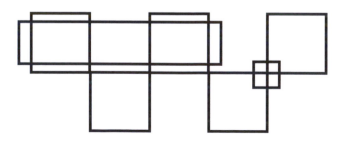

Answers on page 189.

Nokio's Nose Problem

P. Nokio had a problem. Every time he heard a lie, his nose grew an inch. He traveled to Noliarsville, wanting to be surrounded by only honest people so that his nose would stop growing. P. Nokio stepped off the bus in Noliarsville and immediately met 3 of the town's male citizens. He put them to the test, asking each one, "Are you an honest man?" The first man answered, "All I can tell you is that 2 of us are honest men." The second man said, "Only 1 of us is an honest man." The third man said to P. Nokio, "The man who answered before me is an honest man." How many inches, if any, did P. Nokio's nose grow?

Number Fitting

Fill in this crossword with numbers instead of letters. Use the clues to determine which of the digits 1 through 9 belongs in each square. No zeros are used.

Hint: Start by comparing 5–Down and 3–Down, keeping the length of 2–Down in mind.

Across

1. A perfect square
4. The sum of its digits is 18
5. A multiple of 19
6. Consecutive digits, ascending

Down

1. A multiple of 9
2. Four different digits
3. 44 more than 5–Down
5. The square root of 2–Down

Answers on page 189.

Furry Friend

Cryptograms are messages in substitution code. Break the code to read the message. For example, THE SMART CAT might become FVO QWGDF JGF if F is substituted for T, V for H, O for E, and so on.

HLBOVNGK   KIN   (name of animal)

HLBOVNGK   KINV   ICO   MLMXEIC   IV

PLXVOPLEH   MONV.   IEE   KINV   ICO   VBIEE

KICRGTLCLXV   IRGBIEV,   TIEXIFEO   ALC

JGEEGRS   BGKO   IRH   CINV.   KINV   PITO

CONCIKNGEO   KEIUV;   JOOR   POICGRS   IRH

VBOEE;   COBICJIFEO   RGSPN   TGVGLR;   IRH

KLBMIKN,   BXVKXEIC,   IRH   TOCW   VXMMEO

FLHGOV.   KINV   MLVVOVV   ODKOEEORN

BOBLCW   IRH   IR   IMNGNXHO   ALC   EOICRGRS

FW   LFVOCTINGLR   IRH   ODMOCGORKO.

Answer on page 189.

It Adds Up

COMPUTATION   LOGIC

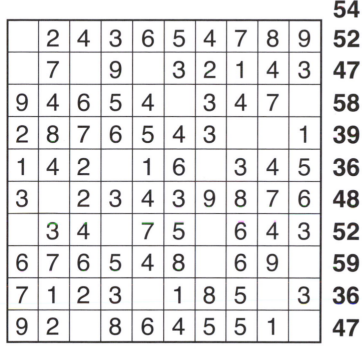

										54
	2	4	3	6	5	4	7	8	9	**52**
	7		9		3	2	1	4	3	**47**
9	4	6	5	4		3	4	7		**58**
2	8	7	6	5	4	3			1	**39**
1	4	2		1	6		3	4	5	**36**
3		2	3	4	3	9	8	7	6	**48**
	3	4		7	5		6	4	3	**52**
6	7	6	5	4	8		6	9		**59**
7	1	2	3		1	8	5		3	**36**
9	2		8	6	4	5	5	1		**47**

55 41 43 52 43 47 55 47 49 42   46

Fill each square in the grid with a digit from 1 to 9. When the numbers in each row are added, you should arrive at the total in the right-hand column. When the numbers in each column are added, you should arrive at the total on the bottom line. The numbers in each diagonal must add up to the totals in the upper and lower right corners.

Lottery Tickets

CREATIVE THINKING   LOGIC

Lou Zer was in charge of the lottery pool at the office. He bought the same number of lottery tickets every week at a dollar apiece. Lou and 9 coworkers each put equal amounts into the pool. One week, 2 people felt unlucky and dropped out, so Lou convinced the rest to put in another dollar so he could still buy the same number of lottery tickets. How many lottery tickets did Lou buy every week?

Answers on page 189.

Where to Find a Cake

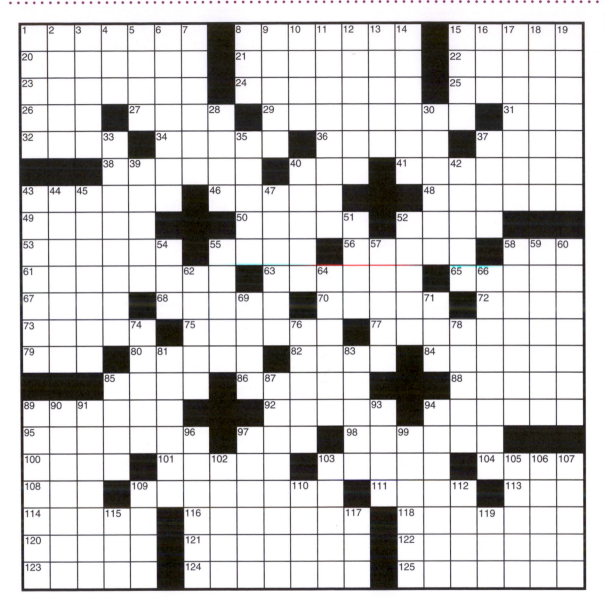

Across

1. Life jacket named for an actress: 2 wds.
8. Paving material
15. Early Peruvians
20. Winnie-the-Pooh creator

21. One way to distribute: Lat., 2 wds.
22. Trunk without a lock
23. Close friends
24. Rushed at
25. Tibet's capital

26. Spicy
27. Fill to excess
29. Hostile
31. Make illegal
32. Linear, briefly: hyph.
34. Spacey of "American Beauty"
36. Easily bribed
37. Tater
38. Accustomed
40. "I've been _____!"
41. Samuel Colt made them
43. Arises unexpectedly: 2 wds.
46. Spot for a mic
48. Location in an Elvis tune
49. Biting
50. Centaur, in part
52. Enjoy some gum
53. Muscle problem
55. Fish dish
56. Didst strike
58. Electronics co.
61. Accept applause: 3 wds.
63. Favored one leg
65. Geo model
67. Apt anagram of vile
68. Former New York governor Mario
70. Big name in racing
72. Bayh of politics
73. Russian revolutionary
75. Characteristics
77. So to speak: 3 wds.
79. Draft org.
80. More off-the-wall
82. Social reformer Jacob
84. Complimentary

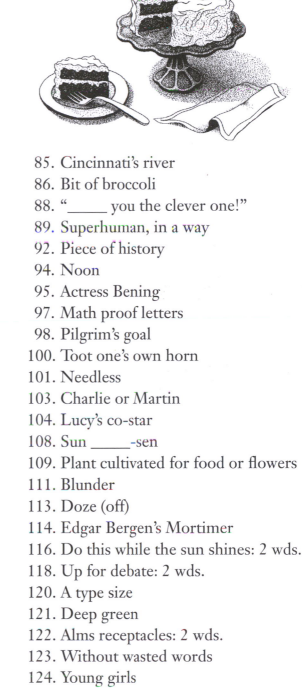

85. Cincinnati's river
86. Bit of broccoli
88. "_____ you the clever one!"
89. Superhuman, in a way
92. Piece of history
94. Noon
95. Actress Bening
97. Math proof letters
98. Pilgrim's goal
100. Toot one's own horn
101. Needless
103. Charlie or Martin
104. Lucy's co-star
108. Sun _____-sen
109. Plant cultivated for food or flowers
111. Blunder
113. Doze (off)
114. Edgar Bergen's Mortimer
116. Do this while the sun shines: 2 wds.
118. Up for debate: 2 wds.
120. A type size
121. Deep green
122. Alms receptacles: 2 wds.
123. Without wasted words
124. Young girls
125. Least taxing

Down

1. Very virile
2. Brother of Moses
3. Overdo the acting
4. Finish first
5. Whitney and Wallach
6. Prepare to pounce: 2 wds.
7. Teacher, at times
8. Base cops, for short
9. "... who _____ heaven": 2 wds.
10. Masked animal, for short
11. They just got here
12. Blocked up
13. Had dinner at home: 2 wds.
14. Zany
15. "_____ never work!"
16. Japanese drama
17. Cage for catching crustaceans: 2 wds.
18. Military offensive
19. Scoundrel: hyph.
28. Stuntman Knievel
30. Hit the runway
33. British Prime Minister Benjamin
35. Tater state
37. Do a slow burn
39. Region of Egypt and Sudan
40. "_____ stand" (Martin Luther): 2 wds.
42. Docile followers
43. Mellow tones
44. Re to re intervals
45. Anthony of "Psycho"
47. Hoi _____
51. Armchair athlete's channel
52. Systems of rules
54. "Today" network
55. Uttered obscenities

57. Flat-topped hills
58. Fastened firmly
59. Russian ruler's wife
60. General pardon
62. Perform better than
64. "Stan the Man" of baseball
66. Given compensation
69. Red planet
71. Oil-drilling machinery
74. Like a rare baseball game: hyph.
76. Out on a limb
78. Prepare for a bout
81. Formal order
83. Kind of whiskey
85. Blood typ.: hyph.
87. Peacocks, e.g.
89. Played the nanny: hyph.
90. Close enough to hit: 2 wds.
91. Out of control: 3 wds.
93. Restaurant employee
94. Small stuff
96. Tooth protector
97. Seismic events
99. Tie in
102. Theatrical performance
103. Oil-yielding rock
105. Come after
106. Minestrone and more
107. That is: Lat., 2 wds.
109. Suffix for chick
110. Bangkok tongue
112. Coal holders
115. ACLU concerns
117. NFL stats
119. Bio. or chem.

Answers on page 190.

Times One Only Once

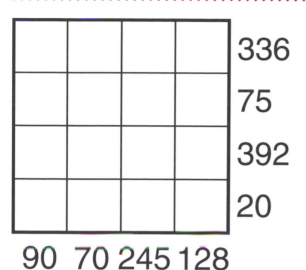

336
75
392
20

90 70 245 128

Fill each square in the grid with a digit from 1 to 9. When the numbers in each row are multiplied, you should arrive at the total in the right-hand column. When the numbers in each column are multiplied, you should arrive at the total on the bottom line. Important: Any digit other than 1 may be repeated in a row or column. You will never repeat 1.

Hint: Factor each product into its component prime numbers.

For example, $245 = 5 \times 7 \times 7$.

Think ABCD Once More

LOGIC

Each row and column contains A, B, C, D, and 2 blank squares. Each letter and number indicator refers to the first or second of the 4 letters encountered when traveling inward. Can you complete the grid?

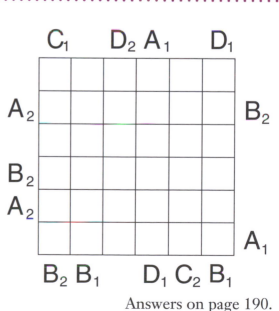

Answers on page 190.

Rhyme Time: Same Game

Answer each clue below with a pair of rhyming words. The numbers that follow each clue indicate how many letters are in each word. For example, "dealer's announcement" would be "same game."

1. Dealer's second announcement (4, 4): <u>SAME GAME</u>

2. Where pleasure craft are displayed (5, 3): _____

3. Gambler's remorse (3, 6): _____

4. Agreeable again (4, 5): _____

5. Win a chef's endurance award (5, 4): _____

6. Locks fix (4, 6): _____

7. Harvest transport (5, 5): _____

8. Ooze black gold (5, 5): _____

9. Seasonal piece of jewelry (6, 4): _____

10. It goes with the badge (6, 5): _____

11. Really neat weightlifter's device (5, 7): _____

12. Where the awards get passed out (6, 6): _____

13. Part of a fish's innards (6, 6): _____

14. Gets greenery (8, 6): _____

15. Household device in a union (9, 8): _____

Answers on page 190.

REASSESS YOUR BRAIN

You have just completed a set of puzzles designed to challenge your various mental skills. We hope you enjoyed them. Did this mental exercise also improve your memory, attention, problem-solving, and other important cognitive skills? To get a sense of your improvement, please fill out this questionnaire. It is exactly the same one you filled out before you worked the puzzles in this book. You can compare your cognitive skills before and after you embarked on a *Brain Games*™ workout.

The following questions will test your skills in the areas of creative thinking, language, and more. Please reflect on each question and rate your responses on a 5-point scale, where 5 equals "excellent" and 1 equals "very poor." Then tally up your scores and check out the categories on the next page to learn how to further sharpen your brain.

1. You're at a party, and you hit it off with someone who could be an important business contact. She gives you her phone number, but you don't have anything to write it down with. How likely are you to remember her phone number?

    1   2   3   4   5

2. How good are you at giving people directions? Do you find that you can explain yourself clearly the first time, or do you frequently need to go back to the beginning and explain directions a different way?

    1   2   3   4   5

3. Consider this situation: You're having a dinner party, and a guest calls at the last minute to ask if he can bring 4 friends who are visiting from out of town. How good are you at juggling your plans to accommodate this unanticipated change?

    1   2   3   4   5

4. How well do you remember the locations of items you use every day, like your keys, cell phone, or wallet? When you need these items, can you locate them easily, or do you have to take time to search for them?

    1   2   3   4   5

5. When you're reading a book or watching a movie, how good is your ability to concentrate? Deduct points if you're easily distracted.

    1   2   3   4   5

6. At work, are you able to efficiently handle more than 1 project at a time, or do you have trouble devoting the necessary attention to each one?

    1   2   3   4   5

7. You buy a new dresser, but assembly is required. When you look at the directions, you find that the illustrations have no written instructions. How good are you at deducing the instructions by interpreting the pictures?

1   2   3   4   5

8. When you go to the grocery store without a list, how good are you at remembering what you need? If you often forget essential items, deduct points accordingly.

1   2   3   4   5

9. How good are your everyday math skills? Are you able to add, subtract, multiply, and divide well in your head?

1   2   3   4   5

10. You receive a bill from your phone company that seems high, but the charges are broken down into complicated categories. You want to have a handle on all the charges before disputing the bill. How good are you at using logic to decipher your monthly statement?

1   2   3   4   5

10–25 Points:

Are You Ready to Make a Change?

Keep at it! There are plenty of activities that will help you improve your brain health. Continue working puzzles on a regular basis. Pick up another *Brain Games*™ book, and choose a different type of puzzle each day, or do a variety of them to help strengthen memory, focus attention, and improve logic and problem-solving.

26–40 Points:

Building Your Mental Muscles

You're no mental slouch, but there's always room to sharpen your mind! Try to identify the types of puzzles that you found particularly difficult in this book. Then you'll get an idea of which cognitive skills you need to work on. Remember, doing a puzzle can be the mental equivalent of doing lunges or squats: While they might not be your first choice of activity, you'll definitely like the results!

41–50 Points:

View from the Top

Congratulations! You have finished the puzzles in this book and are performing like a champion. To maintain this level of mental fitness, keep challenging yourself by working puzzles every day. Like the rest of the body's muscles, your mental strength can decline if you don't use it. So choose to keep your brain strong and active. You're at the summit—now you just have to stay fit to enjoy the view!

ANSWERS

Screwprint: Tracing the Print (page 11)

Hidden Names (page 11)

Al, Mary, Dan, Andy, Phil, Les, Ed, Tom, Matt

Cat Got Your Dog? (page 12)

cat, cot, cog, dog

Find "Ox" (page 12)

While working at Fort KnOX, OttO Xavier put a bOX of rocks in ROXy's in-bOX, hoping to get her attention. ROXy found the bOX when she went to gO XerOX the announcement that she was leaving Fort KnOX to attend OXford on a rowing scholarship as a cOXswain. When he saw the announcement, OttO X-ed out ROXy's name in his Rolodex and turned his attention to MOXy, a fOXy chatterbOX he met at cardio-kickbOXing. (18)

How to Go Through a Stop Sign (page 13)

Dry Your Eyes (page 14)

Don't cry over spilled milk.

Three-Letter Anagrams (page 14)

1. ewe, wee; 2. gum, mug; 3. Pam, map; 4. not, ton; 5. two, tow; 6. Deb, bed

Do the Math (page 15)

First Assembling (page 15)

Inherit the Win (page 16)

Misers aren't much fun to live with but they make great ancestors.

Yardful of Y's (page 17)

1. yacht; 2. yaks; 3. yardstick; 4. yarn; 5. yogurt; 6. yoke; 7. yucca plant

Rhyme Time: Fly By (page 18)

1. fly by; 2. low row; 3. pour more; 4. pool tool; 5. can't plant; 6. score more; 7. mule school; 8. grass class; 9. floor chore; 10. unheard word

Passing a Bird's Home (page 18)

One Flew Over the Cuckoo's Nest

Times Across and Down (page 19)

3	2	1	7	42
5	2	5	1	50
3	1	3	3	27
1	2	5	4	40

45 8 75 84

C-Dissection (page 19)

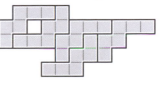

Answers

It Figures (page 20)

			19
2	1	7	**10**
3	4	9	**16**
8	5	6	**19**
13	**10**	**22**	**12**

Sudoku Fun (page 20)

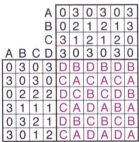

1	2	3	8	7	4	5	6	9
5	6	7	9	3	2	1	8	4
8	4	9	6	5	1	2	3	7
9	1	6	2	4	7	8	5	3
3	5	8	1	9	6	4	7	2
4	7	2	3	8	5	9	1	6
2	9	1	7	6	8	3	4	5
6	8	5	4	2	3	7	9	1
7	3	4	5	1	9	6	2	8

ABCD Numbered (page 22)

			A	0	3	0	3	0	3
			B	0	2	1	2	1	3
			C	3	1	2	1	2	0
A	B	C	D	3	0	3	0	3	0
0	3	0	3	D	B	D	B	D	B
3	0	3	0	C	A	C	A	C	A
0	2	2	2	D	C	B	C	D	B
3	1	1	1	C	A	D	A	B	A
0	3	2	1	D	B	C	B	C	B
3	0	1	2	C	A	D	A	D	A

Good Fortune Maze (page 22)

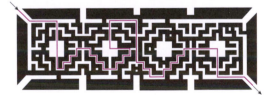

Word Columns (page 23)

Political strategy is when you don't let people know you have run out of ideas and keep shouting anyway.

In the Room (page 23)

Someone

Life's Little Mysteries (page 24)

1. Why do they call it a TV set when you only get one?
2. Why is it that when you transport something by car, it's a shipment, but when you send it by ship, it's called cargo?
3. How does the guy who drives the snowplow get to work in the morning?
4. Can an ambidextrous person make an offhand remark?
5. Why don't they just make food stamps edible?

Fly Away (page 25)

dove, love, lore, lure, lurk, lark

The Hidden Shape (page 25)

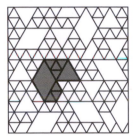

Fitting Words with a G (page 26)

S	P	A	N	K
C	A	J	U	N
A	G	A	T	E
T	E	R	S	E

The Days Are Numbered (page 26)

				17
2	9	2	5	**18**
3	5	1	4	**13**
6	7	2	9	**24**
4	8	3	1	**16**
15	**29**	**8**	**19**	**10**

Number Quest (page 27)

Mosaic Maze (page 28)

The Stars Are Numbered (page 29)

Edible Anagrams (page 29)

1. diary, dairy; 2. sauce, cause; 3. west, stew;
4. last, salt; 5. team, meat

Spin a Web (pages 30–31)

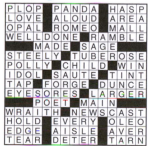

Rhyme Time: Free Me (page 32)

1. free me; 2. dime lime; 3. sent rent; 4. still will;
5. steer here; 6. spell well; 7. spare snare; 8. store
chore; 9. quite trite; 10. normal formal

It's Thrilling (page 32)

Sudden-death overtime

Anagram Pairs (page 33)

1. are, ear; 2. gob, bog; 3. who, how; 4. ode, doe;
5. ten, net; 6. owl, low; 7. ape, pea; 8. Ida, aid;
9. nap, pan; 10. sub, bus

Weather or Not! (page 34)

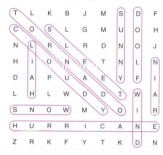

One of the Dwarfs (page 34)

Bashful (half bus)

Spotted Flowers (page 35)

66 dots

Animal Quest (page 35)

Times Down and Across (page 36)

5	2	5	1	50
1	2	3	3	18
5	2	1	2	20
5	1	3	7	105
125	8	45	42	

Answers

Squares Galore! (page 36)

5 squares

Bungle in the Jungle (page 37)

1. Elephant in the tree; 2. Elephant's ears look like wings; 3. Deer behind tree; 4. Penguin in the jungle; 5. Wristwatch on gorilla; 6. Giraffe head on bird; 7. Hunter has half a mustache

More Sudoku Fun (page 38)

2	5	4	3	6	9	1	7	8
9	1	6	2	8	7	4	5	3
8	7	3	1	5	4	2	6	9
1	2	5	7	3	6	8	9	4
4	6	9	8	1	5	7	3	2
3	8	7	4	9	2	5	1	6
6	4	2	9	7	1	3	8	5
5	3	1	6	2	8	9	4	7
7	9	8	5	4	3	6	2	1

Fitting Words with an N (page 39)

P	A	S	S	E
A	L	O	N	E
C	O	R	A	L
K	E	E	P	S

Odds-or-Evens (page 39)

14. Rod won 5 and Steven won 9—5 to cancel out Rod's wins and 4 to win beers.

Rhyme Time: Why Fly (page 40)

1. why fly; 2. why July; 3. box socks; 4. main drain; 5. snore more; 6. hefty lefty; 7. store floor; 8. Norse force; 9. still grill; 10. mother's brothers

On Call (page 40)

J (The first letters on each button on a telephone keypad.)

Season Search (page 41)

[grid of letters with WINTER, AUTUMN, SUMMER, etc. circled]

My Dinner with Andre (page 42)

1. Using a fork backward; 2. Salt and pepper in wrong shakers; 3. Gap in chair leg; 4. Glass of peas; 5. Book on plate instead of food; 6. Tined fork is splayed; 7. Arm through back of chair; 8. Long tie across table; 9. Utensil fingers; 10. Drink spilling up; 11. Hammer

Head to Toes (page 43)

head, read, road, toad, toed, toes

Go for the Gourd (page 43)

GOmer GOt the urge to draG Out an orange GOurd even though it wasn't Halloween. He carved his own face, which shows that his eGO was a biG One. GOmer GOt more GOurds and carved a GOose with GOut, an egG On a wall, and a ganG Of GOrillas GOing ape. He showed them to his gal Gloria, a former GO-GO dancer who was now a biG Old GOurd grower from Georgia. She gave GOmer a baG Of seeds to grow more GOurds and GO whole-hoG Out on his porch carving them. (24)

Food for Thought (page 44)

Hidden message: Each word or expression includes a word that is a type of cake.

Unmistakable Aroma (page 45)

You can't act like a skunk without someone getting wind of it.

Play Sudoku (page 45)

5	3	1	7	6	9	2	4	8
4	2	7	8	3	1	9	5	6
8	6	9	4	2	5	1	7	3
1	8	2	5	4	6	3	9	7
6	4	5	3	9	7	8	2	1
9	7	3	1	8	2	4	6	5
3	5	4	2	7	8	6	1	9
7	9	8	6	1	4	5	3	2
2	1	6	9	5	3	7	8	4

Multiplicity (page 46)

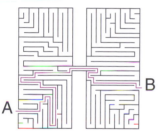

				135
4	4	3	5	240
5	4	3	2	120
5	3	3	1	45
3	4	5	1	60
300	192	135	10	48

Dotted States (page 46)

40 dots

H Is for Help! (page 47)

A
B

Like a Candy Bar (page 47)

Chock full of nuts

Records (pages 48–49)

R	I	A	S		I	D	E	A	S		A	W	A	Y
I	T	C	H		M	I	S	D	O		S	R	T	A
P	U	T	O	N	P	A	P	E	R		S	I	L	L
S	P	I	R	A	L	L	Y		T	O	A	T	E	E
			A	M	O	S		C	E	N	S	E		
L	I	M	N	E	D		C	A	R	E	S	S	E	R
O	D	E		D	E	C	A	L		S	I	D	L	E
L	I	M	O		D	A	R	E	S		N	O	L	I
L	O	O	P	S		K	E	B	A	B		W	I	N
S	T	R	E	A	M	E	D		C	R	A	N	E	S
		A	N	N	A	S		C	R	A	M			
P	A	N	N	E	D		S	H	I	V	E	R	E	D
R	O	D	E		M	A	K	E	S	A	N	O	T	E
O	N	U	S		A	L	I	S	T		D	U	N	E
D	E	M	S		N	A	S	T	Y		S	T	A	R

Rhyme Time: Imp Ump (page 51)

1. imp ump; 2. plum gum; 3. mule fuel; 4. sled shed; 5. heel deal; 6. bored lord; 7. royal toil; 8. waste paste; 9. great debate; 10. freight rate

Mind-Bender (page 51)

Write this message backward and respace. You'll then read: "Stifle is an anagram of itself."

Numbers in a Crossword (page 52)

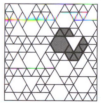

2	3	4	
6	7	6	
	7	8	4
	3	2	9

Another Hidden Shape (page 52)

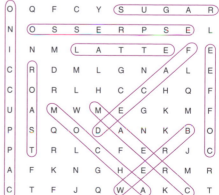

Rhyming Duos (page 53)

1. weights and measures; 2. wax and wane; 3. off and on; 4. his and hers; 5. horse and buggy; 6. hit and run; 7. man and wife; 8. fast and loose; 9. short and sweet; 10. shoes and socks

Special Number (page 53)

The 10 digits in this number appear in alphabetical order.

Caffeinated (page 54)

Answers

Word Columns (page 55)

In some societies, they beat the ground with clubs and yell. It is called witchcraft. Other societies call it "golf."

Back at You (page 55)

A mirror

From A to Z (page 56)

Dr. Don't-Dare! (page 56)

1. Balloons attached to oxygen tank; 2. Feather in the doctor's cap; 3. Doctors with arms around each other; 4. Coke IV; 5. Cat in the operating room; 6. Mouse in the operating room; 7. Nurse wearing a football helmet; 8. Surgeon wearing a hard hat; 9. Surgeon operating with wire cutters; 10. Patient awake; 11. Pack of cigarettes on the instrument table; 12. Nurse not wearing surgical gown

Around the House (page 57)

Times It! (page 58)

3	6	1	7	126
3	1	5	9	135
1	2	5	7	70
3	2	5	1	30
27	24	125	441	

Triangles Within Triangles (page 58)

13 triangles

Word-Surfin' Safari (page 59)

The hidden animals are underlined below. In order, they are: jackal, raven, cow, camel, ass, frog, cat, hare, fish, mule, bat, goat, bear, hen, sheep, serpent, lamb, gull, lion, crow, dog, beagle, eagle, wolf, calf.

Jack, a likable wizard, even if a bit of a craven coward, came looking for a pretty lass. He paced to and fro, getting more agitated by the moment. "This is a catastrophe!" he wailed. "The town is full of women, but which are the ones for me? They seem so standoffish." He rubbed the magic amulet on a leather strap around his neck. He wore it always, even when bathing. "I've got to go at it, just keep looking, but this is unbearable! When will I find her?" He tried shouting his favorite magical incantations—"Banshee pickles!" and "Hairdresser pentagon!" and "Bedlam boogie!"—but they had no effect at all. He didn't want his epitaph to read "Here Lies Jack, the Wizard of Lonely," he thought, popping a sad little Meal-for-One of Slumgullion Stew into the microwave. Later, he took his dog, a beagle named Wolfgang, for a long walk. As Wolfgang stopped to leave his calling card with a fire hydrant, another dog appeared. Unlikely as it seemed, a comely owner was at the other end of its leash. Even more surprising, she had a friendly smile. The 2 dog-lovers got to chatting, and then, ever so casually, Jack found himself strolling along the sidewalk with his new acquaintance while their pets frolicked. Need we add that this comical farce had a happy ending?

Find "Now" (page 60)

During the sNOWstorm, Howard played UNO With Zowie, not kNOWing when the sNOW-storm would end. UnbekNOWnst to Howard, Zowie had NO Worries about winning because she kNOWs how to palm Uno cards. Losing badly, Howard had a plaN. "OW!" he yelled, pretending to get a paper cut and sending the cards from UNO Whirling to the floor. "NOW you've done it," yelled Zowie, and she donned her sNOWshoes and left, kNOWing Howard had figured her out. (12)

A Sudoku Treat (page 60)

8	4	7	2	5	3	6	9	1
3	6	2	7	1	9	4	5	8
5	9	1	8	4	6	2	7	3
4	1	8	3	9	5	7	2	6
7	3	5	6	2	8	1	4	9
6	2	9	1	7	4	8	3	5
2	5	3	4	8	1	9	6	7
9	8	4	5	6	7	3	1	2
1	7	6	9	3	2	5	8	4

More Than a Word (page 61)

```
A S Y G C T B N O N T
Y M F R R A O D O A R
  I S U R S O R H H N E
L E G B D K E A A S T S V A C N T
T H M E A R C H W T S U L O A E T
M R O E U D C A U R L W A U N E A
E I A N A I N O N G E R E I O N S
L L N N R N B E A S S C L I Y F S
D E I R K A I R W E Y E R A G A O
R I O F Y A L N C B V T D U R H M
R O R R O A N L C I E N L E I E T
P O R T T R O D S O O A N A T T H
I O U I Y T P N F M M O R N S G E
S L N G H R E W E I M E S S E B E
  G H F I U O M L I N S
  E F I L C O L A E C H
  O P B T C E H R A S E
```

In a Stew (page 62)

carrot, turnip, pasta, potato, seasoning, leek, chicken, celery

Fire Figures (page 62)

There are 4 firefighters and 3 fire trucks.

Bank Shot (page 63)

I ain't saying the customer service in my bank is bad, but when I went in the other day and asked the clerk to check my balance, she leaned over and pushed me.

X Marks the Spot! (page 63)

						30
9	3	5	4	7	3	31
2	1	2	8	2	8	23
1	6	4	1	9	3	24
7	3	7	2	1	6	26
4	9	8	6	4	5	36
8	5	9	5	7	1	35
31	27	35	26	30	26	21

Summertime Fun (pages 64–65)

C	E	D	E		A	Y	E		L	A	S	S
B	A	I	L		L	A	P		E	L	I	A
S	U	N	S	H	I	N	E		M	E	N	U
		G	E	E		K	E	R	O	U	A	C
T	A	B		R	U	E		U	N	T	I	E
S	L	A	V		S	E	P	I	A			
P	E	T	A	L	S		F	N	D	E	A	N
			C	O	R	E	R		E	X	P	O
A	M	M	A	N		A	U	G		P	E	T
B	O	O	T	E	E	S		A	O	L		
A	C	T	I		S	E	A	S	H	O	R	E
S	H	O	O		A	L	B		O	R	A	L
E	A	R	N		U	S	E		H	E	N	S

Spinning in Circles (page 66)

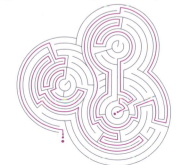

Answers

Begin Play (page 66)
Underhand serve

Rhyme Time: Wet Pet (page 67)
1. wet pet; 2. let bet; 3. bare hair; 4. near beer;
5. nice mice; 6. dine fine; 7. doc's socks; 8. Rhine
wine; 9. share hair; 10. relay delay

Seasoned (page 67)
L (NaCl is the chemical formula for sodium
chloride, or salt.)

Thinking Outside the Bubbles (page 68)
Thanksgiving

Fitting Words with an A (page 68)

M	A	R	S	H
E	X	I	L	E
O	L	D	E	R
W	E	E	D	S

Ticket to Ride (page 69)
1. cae sar ean; 2. dra gon fly; 3. tim epi ece;
sar + gon + epi = Singapore

Unique Location (page 69)

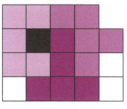

Ten-Five, Good Buddy (page 70)
1. Hitchhiker in tree; 2. Deer head in tree trunk;
3. Branch growing out of truck; 4. Company
name runs off end of truck; 5. Missing back
wheels; 6. Driver on wrong side; 7. Missing
headlight; 8. Tree is growing in the middle of the
road; 9. Pie in the sky

Sudoku Rules (page 71)

2	9	8	3	6	7	4	1	5
5	3	1	9	4	8	7	2	6
4	7	6	5	1	2	3	8	9
9	8	5	6	2	4	1	3	7
7	2	3	8	5	1	9	6	4
6	1	4	7	9	3	2	5	8
3	6	7	2	8	9	5	4	1
8	4	2	1	7	5	6	9	3
1	5	9	4	3	6	8	7	2

Go Forth and Multiply! (page 71)

			24
4	1	3	12
2	4	5	40
2	3	1	6
16	12	15	16

Four-Letter Anagrams (page 72)
1. sway, ways; 2. emit, time; 3. tend, dent;
4. mope, poem; 5. Edna, Dane; 6. eels, else;
7. none, neon; 8. Nile, line; 9. ages, sage;
10. tarp, part

Travel Trouble (page 72)
Bob and Rob are twins from Siam but not con-
joined twins.

Zen in a Nutshell (page 73)
Be here now. Be someplace else later. Is that so
complicated?

Triangles Galore! (page 73)
14 triangles

Fitting Words with an M (page 74)

Q	U	A	F	F
U	N	T	I	L
A	D	O	R	E
D	O	M	E	D

So Many Books (page 74)
read, road, rood, rook, book

A Matter of Faith (page 75)

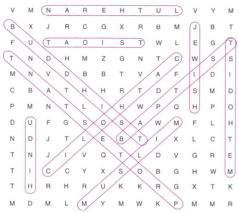

Creature Corner (pages 76–77)

Family Vacation (page 78)

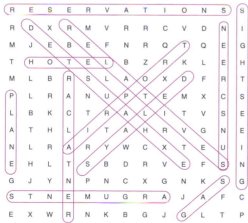

Rhyme Time: Slow Flow (page 79)

1. slow flow; 2. fish dish; 3. play away; 4. sole goal; 5. full bull; 6. pail tale; 7. worn horn; 8. wide slide; 9. ghost host; 10. third word; 11. horse force; 12. border order; 13. madder adder; 14. better letter; 15. colder shoulder

Circular Reasoning (page 80)

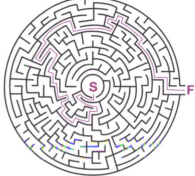

How's the Weather? (page 80)

O (The Rain in Spain Falls Mainly on the Plain.)

World Capitals (page 81)

A-D; B-L; C-B; D-M; E-H; F-O; G-J; H-N; I-A; J-P; K-R; L-G; M-C; N-I; O-E; P-K; R-T; S-W; T-Y; U-S.

1. Oslo, Norway; 2. Stockholm, Sweden; 3. New Delhi, India; 4. Cairo, Egypt; 5. Belgrade, Serbia; 6. Amsterdam, Netherlands; 7. Madrid, Spain; 8. Tokyo, Japan; 9. Santiago, Chile; 10. Phnom Penh, Cambodia

Tricky Codeword Puzzle (page 83)

Answers

Sittin' on Top of the World (pages 84-85)
1. b; 2. false; 3. c; 4. false; 5. a; 6. a; 7. true; 8. b; 9. false; 10. c

Star Power (page 85)

Spotted Tools (page 86)
53 dots

ABCD Challenge (page 86)

	A B C D					
A	1	3	0	3	1	1
B	3	1	1	1	3	0
C	0	2	2	0	2	3
A B C D	2	0	3	2	0	2

A B C D							
3	2	0	1	B	A	D	A	B	A
2	1	2	1	A	B	C	D	A	C
1	0	2	3	D	C	D	A	C	D
1	2	2	1	B	A	C	D	B	C
0	1	2	3	D	C	D	B	C	D
2	3	1	0	B	A	B	A	B	C

Gaggle of G's (page 87)
1. galoshes; 2. garbage; 3. garbage can; 4. gin rummy; 5. glasses ; 6. gloves; 7. goatee; 8. goblet; 9. goldfish; 10. goldfish bowl; 11. golf bag; 12. golf clubs; 13. gorilla; 14. grandfather clock; 15. grapes

Rules of Thumb (page 88)
1. Energy: One BTU equals roughly the energy of one average candy bar or one blue-tip wooden match. 2. Poker rule: Look around the table and find the victim. If you can't tell who it is, it's you. 3. How to mix a proper oil-and-vinegar salad dressing: Three parts oil, one part vinegar. 4. What to bring to summer camp: A good rule of thumb? If you care about the item, leave it at home.

Sleigh Bells (page 88)
C (Dasher, Dancer, Prancer, Vixen, Comet, Cupid, Donder, Blitzen)

Why Oh Why Do I Multiply? (page 89)

					16
4	4	4	3	1	192
5	4	3	2	1	120
3	3	2	2	5	180
5	1	2	2	5	100
4	3	5	1	2	120
1200	144	240	24	50	128

Chill! (page 89)
warm, ward, card, cord, cold

Deli Misadventures (pages 90-91)

Sudoku Rules Once More (page 92)

5	1	8	7	6	9	3	2	4
3	6	9	4	2	8	5	7	1
7	2	4	5	3	1	8	6	9
1	8	3	2	9	7	6	4	5
2	7	5	8	4	6	9	1	3
4	9	6	3	1	5	2	8	7
9	5	2	1	8	4	7	3	6
8	4	7	6	5	3	1	9	2
6	3	1	9	7	2	4	5	8

Easy as ABC (page 92)

Word Columns (page 93)

Feeling pity for the lobsters in the tank at the restaurant, the crook broke in at night and released them in the forest.

Crooks in a Row (page 93)

Police lineup

Play Ball! (page 94)

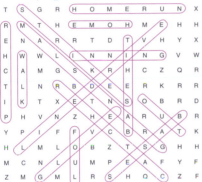

Get Smart! (page 95)

Barnard, Bryn Mawr, Mount Holyoke, Radcliffe, Smith, Vassar, Wellesley
Unscrambled phrase: The Seven Sisters
(These Ivy League-related colleges are known as "The Seven Sisters.")

Vitamin Vic (page 95)

The potatoes. Vic eats only things that grow on vines.

President's Maxim (page 96)

You can fool some of the people all of the time, and all of the people some of the time, but you cannot fool all of the people all of the time.

—Abraham Lincoln

Rhyme Time: Soft Loft (page 97)

1. soft loft; 2. mock block; 3. lack black; 4. base place; 5. exalt salt; 6. paste waste; 7. raven haven; 8. swell smell; 9. broth cloth; 10. create great; 11. change range; 12. center renter; 13. locket pocket; 14. leather tether; 15. boomer consumer

NASCAR Family (pages 98–99)

M	I	S	S	A	L		D	U	S	T	E	D
U	N	H	O	L	Y		O	R	I	O	L	E
S	T	U	P	O	R		C	I	T	R	I	C
E	R	N		T	E	S	T		S	O	S	A
D	O	T	E			T	O	P		N	I	N
		R	E	T	I	R	E		T	O	T	
R	A	C	E	R	E	L	A	T	I	O	N	S
E	N	O		M	A	L	L	E	T			
C	A	N		A	P	E		S	M	E	E	
O	H	N	O		A	R	C	H		E	M	U
R	E	I	N	E	R		H	O	T	A	I	R
D	I	V	E	R	T		A	P	O	L	L	O
S	M	E	A	R	Y		T	E	N	S	E	S

Solve Logidoku (page 99)

5	8	7	1	6	3	4	2
4	1	3	6	2	7	5	8
3	2	4	5	8	1	6	7
7	6	2	8	4	5	1	3
6	4	5	3	7	8	2	1
1	3	6	7	5	2	8	4
2	7	8	4	1	6	3	5
8	5	1	2	3	4	7	6

It's a Wrap! (page 100)

B

Numbered Stars (page 100)

Answers

And in Summary (page 101)

							47
1	4	3	2	1	2	8	21
7	2	6	5	4	9	3	36
8	9	3	1	8	2	3	34
4	5	3	4	7	1	8	32
3	6	7	1	5	4	3	29
2	6	1	4	8	6	1	28
5	4	3	6	4	9	7	38
30	36	26	23	37	33	33	28

Party Dress (page 101)

We know that no one was wearing a dress to match her name. Since Magenta agreed with the woman in the teal dress, that means the woman in the teal dress was Hazel. It then follows that Magenta was wearing the hazel dress, and Teal was in the magenta dress.

Rhyme Time: Test Rest (page 102)

1. test rest; 2. sell well; 3. free brie; 4. sock stock; 5. long sarong; 6. ruddy buddy; 7. mixer fixer; 8. large charge; 9. caddie daddy; 10. duller color; 11. simple dimple; 12. bought naught; 13. fender bender; 14. greater crater; 15. merrier terrier

Square Grid (page 103)

5	4	1
1	4	9
2	1	6

All Aboard (page 103)

Constrained (second train)

Winter Wonders (pages 104–105)

W	A	S		O	H	M	S		L	O	A	M
A	N	T		R	E	A	P		E	L	S	E
S	N	O	W	B	A	L	L	F	I	G	H	T
P	A	P	A		D	E	A	R		A	Y	E
		H	A	W			T	I	P			
A	L	A		G	A	S		G	A	F	F	E
H	O	C	K	E	Y	P	L	A	Y	E	R	S
S	T	E	E	L		Y	E	T		D	O	T
			G	E	M		O	E	R			
E	T	A		S	O	A	P		A	U	N	T
C	H	R	I	S	T	M	A	S	T	R	E	E
R	O	I	L		T	Y	R	O		G	S	A
U	R	A	L		O	L	D	S		E	S	S

Wave of W's (page 106)

1. wall; 2. wastebasket; 3. wastepaper; 4. watch; 5. watering can; 6. weather vane; 7. web; 8. weeds; 9. whiskers; 10. wicker chair; 11. windmill; 12. wine; 13. wineglass; 14. woodpile

Arrow Web (page 107)

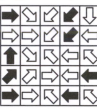

Logidoku in Shapes (page 107)

3	7	6	4	2	8	1	5
2	8	7	3	5	1	6	4
5	6	1	8	3	4	2	7
1	4	2	5	7	6	8	3
6	3	8	2	4	7	5	1
7	5	3	1	6	2	4	8
4	1	5	6	8	3	7	2
8	2	4	7	1	5	3	6

Give Sudoku a Shot (page 109)

8	1	6	2	9	4	3	5	7
5	4	3	7	1	8	2	6	9
7	9	2	6	3	5	1	4	8
4	3	8	5	7	6	9	1	2
1	7	5	9	4	2	8	3	6
6	2	9	3	8	1	4	7	5
9	6	4	1	2	7	5	8	3
2	8	7	4	5	3	6	9	1
3	5	1	8	6	9	7	2	4

Give Logidoku a Shot (page 109)

SUMsational! (page 110)

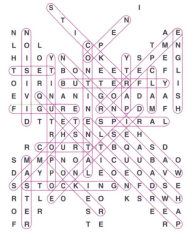

Time Off (page 110)

work, pork, perk, peak, peat, plat, play

May We Have a (Weird) Word With You? (page 111)

1. fruitless; 2. precaution; 3. kidnapping;
4. humanitarian; 5. interstates

Fitting Words with a C (page 112)

P	A	G	A	N
O	B	E	S	E
T	U	N	I	C
S	T	E	A	K

B-Dissection (page 112)

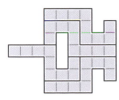

Rhyme Time: Wind Kind (page 113)

1. wind kind; 2. hard yard; 3. warm dorm; 4. tram scam; 5. pork fork; 6. rare chair; 7. regal eagle; 8. sweet treat; 9. troupe group; 10. groovy movie; 11. dental rental; 12. skeeter meter

Before and After (pages 114–115)

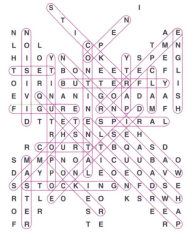

1. butterfly; 2. clam; 3. continental; 4. court;
5. distance; 6. division; 7. double; 8. emperor;
9. English; 10. figure; 11. master; 12. open;
13. opportunity; 14. party; 15. perfect; 16. poker;
17. question; 18. spiral; 19. squash; 20. sticker;
21. stocking; 22. test; 23. Thomas; 24. Washington.
Leftover letters spell: In all those before-and-after ads, nobody ever looks worse after.

Time for Grooming (page 116)

51 dots

Counting Candy (page 116)

Andy has to give Randy 40 more pieces of candy, then each will have 120 pieces. At the start Andy had 180 pieces and Randy had 60.

Deal! (page 117)

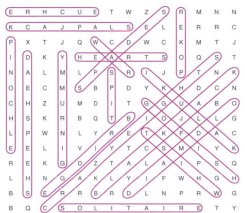

Answers

Instant Cure (page 118)

When I told my doctor I couldn't afford an operation, he offered to touch-up my X-rays.
—Henny Youngman

Think ABCD (page 118)

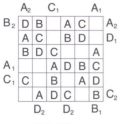

Sum Box (page 119)

$7+7+7+4=25$

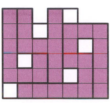

Try Another Logidoku Challenge (page 119)

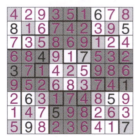

Gram's Birthday (pages 120–121)

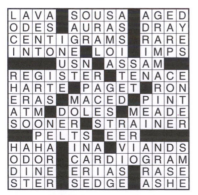

The Answer Man (pages 122–123)

1. The President of the United States had the same name in 1980 that he has today. Told you it was a trick question! 2. Eddie didn't write the book, Invictus did; 3. Milwaukee; 4. 42

Easy to Do (page 123)

Piece of cake

Crisscross Puzzle (page 124)

Move the Matchsticks (page 125)

$V \times X = L$ (Roman numerals)

Tennis Aces (page 125)

Roddick is ahead 1–0 in the fourth set but down 2 sets to 1. With 5 points in the third set tiebreak game, he served 2 aces to win the set. Then he served the first game of the fourth set with 4 more aces.

Rhyme Time: Top Crop (page 126)

1. top crop; 2. try thigh; 3. pipe type; 4. cool pool; 5. mall stall; 6. small ball; 7. stale mail; 8. stash cash; 9. faint taint; 10. clock stock; 11. hokey pokey; 12. green marine; 13. light flight; 14. horse course; 15. better setter

Answers

ABCD with a C (page 127)

		A	3	0	0	2	2	2
		B	0	3	2	1	2	1
		C	1	3	2	1	1	1
A	B	C D	2	0	2	2	1	2

2	2	1	1	A	B	C	A	B	D
1	1	2	2	D	C	B	D	A	C
3	2	0	1	A	B	D	A	B	A
1	1	1	3	D	C	B	D	A	D
0	3	3	0	C	B	C	B	C	B
2	0	2	2	A	C	D	C	D	A

A Sudoku Enigma (page 127)

8	4	7	2	1	9	6	5	3
2	5	3	4	7	6	8	1	9
9	1	6	3	8	5	2	4	7
3	8	9	7	6	1	5	2	4
7	6	5	9	2	4	1	3	8
4	2	1	8	5	3	7	9	6
1	7	4	5	9	8	3	6	2
6	9	8	1	3	2	4	7	5
5	3	2	6	4	7	9	8	1

Nation of N's (page 128)

1. nail; 2. nail file; 3. nautilus; 4. nectarines;
5. necks; 6. necktie; 7. net; 8. newspaper;
9. noses; 10. notes; 11. nuts; 12. nutcracker

Word Columns (page 129)

No one knew who was attacking the castle until we learned it was the forces of Sir Nymbas of Cumulus, the legendary Dark and Stormy Knight.

Count Me In! (page 130)

								42
2	3	1	2	8	4	6	2	28
1	4	6	4	6	5	1	8	35
6	2	5	8	6	9	3	5	44
7	8	2	7	4	7	8	6	49
4	3	1	5	6	7	5	1	32
5	7	6	6	7	8	6	5	50
3	8	1	3	6	4	9	3	37
7	2	4	2	5	1	2	1	24
35	37	26	37	48	45	40	31	42

Rectangles in Mass (page 130)

There are 31 rectangles in the drawing.

Geometric Shapes (page 131)

Three for Two (page 131)

1. <u>carrot</u>, es<u>carg</u>ot; 2. <u>Erie</u>, Super<u>ior</u>;
3. Sept<u>ember</u>, Nov<u>ember</u>, Dec<u>ember</u>; 4. Sa<u>hara</u>,
Kala<u>hari</u>; 5. Hun<u>gary</u>, Bul<u>gary</u>a

M Is for Mystery (page 132)

Man of Steel Chalet = The Maltese Falcon; Hag at Charities = Agatha Christie; Our Helicopter = Hercule Poirot; Simple Arms = Miss Marple; My Spiderwort Eel = Lord Peter Wimsey; Guinea Dustup = Auguste Dupin; Glad Aeroplane = Edgar Allan Poe; Chilean Arch = Charlie Chan; Give yourself bonus points if your keen deductive powers revealed Shellshock Rome as Sherlock Holmes, whose devoted friend, Two-Star Condo, was his chronicler, Doctor Watson.

Another Fitting Words with a G (page 133)

H	E	D	G	E
A	V	E	R	T
M	I	M	I	C
S	L	O	T	H

On the Right Track (page 133)

plane, plant, plait, plain, blain, brain, train

Answers

Cole Porter Songs (pages 134–135)

Crypto-Animal Families (page 136)

Codes:

1. A-C, B-I, C-G, D-N, E-O, F-A, G-R, H-E, I-S, J-W, K-T, M-H, N-K, O-D, P-U, R-L, S-P, T-B.
2. A-P, B-F, C-B, D-M, E-H, F-I, G-O, H-T, I-A, J-U, K-S, L-R, M-N, N-E, O-L, P-G, R-Z, S-K.
3. A-T, B-R, C-E, D-G, E-A, F-W, G-U, H-I, I-S, J-Y, K-N, L-H, M-O, N-P, P-L, R-D, S-B, T-F, U-J, V-K.

Answers:

1. Chicken, goat, cow, horse, goose, duckling, sheep, swine, rabbit, hound.
2. Hippopotamus, rhino, tiger, giraffe, elephant, gorilla, zebra, kangaroo, snakes, lion.
3. Whale, seal, turtle, stingray, dolphin, lobster, oyster, starfish, jellyfish, shark.

Psychics for Hire (page 137)

None. It's impossible to only predict 4 out of 5 because that means they would automatically know that the 1 stock left is in the fifth drawer; they would actually have predicted 5 out of 5.

A Capital Puzzle! (page 137)

"Hidden in plain sight" in each sentence is a U.S. state capital. They can be hard to find even when you know what to look for!
1. Lansing (MI); 2. Topeka (KS); 3. Denver (CO); 4. Salem (OR); 5. Boston (MA)

A Logidoku Enigma (page 138)

8	2	1	4	3	7	5	6	9
9	3	6	5	2	1	4	8	7
7	5	4	8	6	9	1	2	3
2	9	8	1	7	4	6	3	5
1	6	3	2	5	8	9	7	4
5	4	7	3	9	6	2	1	8
4	8	2	9	1	3	7	5	6
3	7	5	6	4	2	8	9	1
6	1	9	7	8	5	3	4	2

Adding Is Fun (page 138)

						21
1	3	6	8	6	4	28
4	7	1	9	3	5	29
6	4	2	5	7	7	31
9	5	2	8	2	8	34
2	6	1	5	3	1	18
1	3	8	4	7	9	32
23	28	20	39	28	34	30

Lots of Dots in Gardening (page 139)

100 dots

Don't Answer (page 139)

Beat around the bush

Europe Is Calling Me! (pages 140–141)

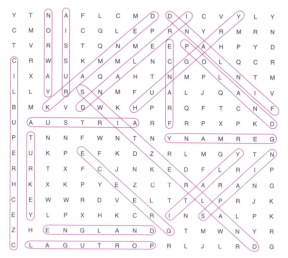

186

Lottery Logic (page 142)

Joe reached into his pocket and pulled out 2 more dollar bills. He added them to the pot, making the total $36. Then the pot could be divided. Gary got one half of $36, or $18. Hurley got one third of $36, or $12. Joe got one ninth of $36, or $4. $18 + $12 + $4 = $34. Joe took the leftover $2 and put it back in his pocket.

Drop Me a Line (page 142)

fish, wish, wise, wine, wink, wonk, honk, hook

Throng of T's (page 143)

1. tea; 2. tea bag; 3. teacup; 4. teapot; 5. teddy bear; 6. telescope; 7. ties (curtain); 8. toast; 9. toes; 10. toothbrush; 11. tot; 12. train; 13. tray; 14. tree; 15. trumpet; 16. trunk; 17. turtle

A Super Logidoku Challenge (page 144)

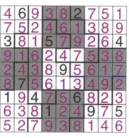

4	6	9	3	8	2	7	5	1
7	5	2	4	6	1	3	8	9
3	8	1	5	7	9	2	6	4
9	1	6	2	4	7	5	3	8
2	4	3	8	9	5	6	1	7
8	7	5	6	1	3	4	9	2
1	9	4	7	5	6	8	2	3
6	3	8	1	2	4	9	7	5
5	2	7	9	3	8	1	4	6

Famed Fabulist (page 144)

This man was, by tradition, a slave who lived in mid-sixth century (Ñ Ñancient Greece. His stories are still taught as moral lessons. Some of his most familiar stories are "The Tortoise and the Hare" and "The Boy Who Cried Wolf." He is known as Aesop.

A Digitized Crossword (page 145)

3	7		3	1
2	3	4	5	6
	1	5	6	
8	7	6	5	4
1	3		3	9

Equalizing Heads (page 145)

Separate the coins into group A with 8 coins and group B with 15 coins. If there are x heads in group A, then there will be 15–x heads in group B. Turn over all coins in group B, and then each group will have x coins facing heads up.

Tourist Attraction (page 146)

1. Dover; 2. inert; 3. singer; 4. nectar; 5. elbow; 6. Yemen; 7. wordy; 8. olive; 9. Rhine; 10. loiter; 11. decal; Tourist Attraction: Disney World

Word Columns (page 147)

My wife insists on putting those little yard lights down both sides of the front sidewalk. Last night a plane tried to land on it and trashed my pink flamingos.

Sudoku on the Brain (page 148)

6	2	1	8	5	7	4	9	3
3	4	9	2	6	1	5	7	8
5	7	8	3	4	9	6	2	1
8	9	2	7	3	6	1	5	4
7	1	6	5	9	4	3	8	2
4	3	5	1	8	2	9	6	7
2	6	3	9	1	8	7	4	5
1	8	4	6	7	5	2	3	9
9	5	7	4	2	3	8	1	6

Try an Odd-Even Logidoku (page 148)

4	8	5	6	3	2	9	1	7
2	6	1	7	9	5	8	4	3
7	9	3	1	8	4	6	5	2
9	1	6	2	7	3	4	8	5
8	7	2	4	5	9	3	6	1
5	3	4	8	6	1	2	7	9
6	5	9	3	1	8	7	2	4
3	2	8	5	4	7	1	9	6
1	4	7	9	2	6	5	3	8

Math—The Final Frontier (page 149)

53

1	7	8	9	1	3	7	1	4	41
6	2	7	4	6	8	2	9	3	47
5	7	4	1	3	2	7	2	5	36
8	2	3	8	2	4	1	9	4	41
9	2	6	9	4	9	5	1	4	49
3	1	3	7	1	9	2	5	3	34
1	2	4	7	2	3	5	7	8	39
5	8	5	4	5	6	1	2	5	41
6	3	6	7	9	8	1	6	1	47
44	34	46	56	33	52	31	42	37	36

Answers

Rating the Guys (page 149)

Antonio is a 12. The dating service rates each guy by giving him 3 points for each syllable in his name.

Angry Prosecutor (pages 150–151)

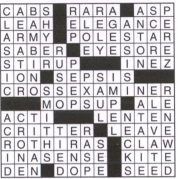

Rhyme Time: Why Try (page 153)

1. why try; 2. stew crew; 3. rich witch; 4. time crime; 5. ford board; 6. swell bell; 7. clock lock; 8. brunch bunch; 9. clever lever; 10. coerce verse; 11. muzzle puzzle; 12. beneath teeth; 13. never endeavor; 14. after laughter; 15. boring flooring

Dan Shocker! (page 154)

Sneaking Brew = Breaking News; New Actress = Newscaster; Banded Cacti = Bad Accident; Toys R Us—EXT XII = Route Sixty-Six; Heroic Pelt = Helicopter; Chipper Sox = Chopper Six; Fired-Up Fat Cat = Traffic Update; Grouchier Ant = Court Hearing; Creole Gave Notice = Election Coverage; Art-Deco Bras = Broadcaster; Cured Pro = Producer; Irate Town Clerk = Walter Cronkite; Sea-Otter Fury = Feature Story.

Know Your Numbers (page 154)

3	9	■	
1	2	1	1
4	9	3	2
■		6	1

Find the Shape (page 155)

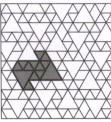

Fitting Words with a P (page 155)

C	O	M	B	S
A	V	E	R	T
M	A	N	I	A
P	L	U	M	B

Push for the Pinnacle (page 156)

5
4 1
7 7 4
2 5 2 2
3 9 6 6 6
2 1 8 8 8 8
3 9 2 6 2 6 2
1 2 7 5 1 1 5 7
8 3 9 8 7 4 7 8 9
2 6 7 2 6 1 3 4 4 5

Horrific Riders (page 156)

D. Pestilence, War, Famine, DEATH (Four Horsemen of the Apocalypse)

The Final Sudoku Challenge (page 157)

6	7	5	1	8	3	4	2	9
2	8	3	9	5	4	1	6	7
9	1	4	2	7	6	3	5	8
1	4	7	5	3	2	8	9	6
3	2	8	6	1	9	7	4	5
5	6	9	8	4	7	2	1	3
8	3	2	4	6	5	9	7	1
7	9	6	3	2	1	5	8	4
4	5	1	7	9	8	6	3	2

The Final Logidoku Challenge (page 157)

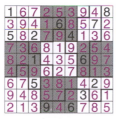

Potpourri of P's (page 158)

1. pail; 2. paint; 3. paintbrush; 4. panes; 5. patch (eye); 6. pearls; 7. pen; 8. pianist; 9. piano; 10. pierced ear; 11. pies; 12. pince-nez; 13. pirate; 14. policeman; 15. precipitation; 16. puddle; 17. pumpkin

Touchdown! (page 159)

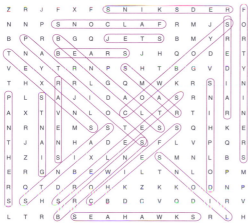

All the World's a Stage (page 160)

drama, drams, crams, clams, slams, shams, shags, stags, stage

A Shapely Challenge (page 160)

41 quadrilaterals

Nokio's Nose Problem (page 161)

Three inches. The second and third men contradict each other, making them both liars, which means that the first man's statement is also a lie.

Number Fitting (page 161)

Furry Friend (page 162)

A-F; B-M; C-R; D-X; E-L; F-B; G-I; H-D; I-A; J-K; K-C; L-O; M-P; N-T; O-E; P-H; R-N; S-G; T-V; U-W; V-S; W-Y; X-U.

Domestic Cat

Domestic cats are popular as household pets. All cats are small carnivorous animals, valuable for killing mice and rats. Cats have retractile claws; keen hearing and smell; remarkable night vision; and compact, muscular, and very supple bodies. Cats possess excellent memory and an aptitude for learning by observation and experience.

It Adds Up (page 163)

										54
4	2	4	3	6	5	4	7	8	9	52
8	7	6	9	4	3	2	1	4	3	47
9	4	6	5	4	8	3	4	7	8	58
2	8	7	6	5	4	3	2	1	1	39
1	4	2	2	1	6	8	3	4	5	36
3	3	2	3	4	3	9	8	7	6	48
6	3	4	8	7	5	6	6	4	3	52
6	7	6	5	4	8	7	6	9	1	59
7	1	2	3	2	1	8	5	4	3	36
9	2	4	8	6	4	5	5	1	3	47
55	41	43	52	43	47	55	47	49	42	46

Lottery Tickets (page 163)

40. Each person put in $4. When 2 dropped out, there was only $32 in the pot, so each chipped in another $1 to add $8 and bring the total to $40.

Answers

Where to Find a Cake (pages 164–166)

```
MAEWEST MACADAM INCAS
AAMILNE PRORATA TORSO
CRONIES STORMED LHASA
HOT SATE INIMICAL BAN
ONED KEVIN VENAL SPUD
  INURED HAD PISTOLS
POPSUP LAPEL   GHETTO
ACERB  HORSE CHEW
STRAIN SOLE SMOTE RCA
TAKEABOW LIMPED PRIZM
EVIL CUOMO UNSER EVAN
LENIN TRAITS ASITWERE
SSS ODDER RIIS GRATIS
  OHIO SPEAR   ARENT
BIONIC   RELIC MIDDAY
ANNETTE QED SHRINE
BRAG UNDUE SHEEN DESI
YAT AMARANTH FLUB NOD
SNERD MAKEHAY ATISSUE
AGATE EMERALD TINCUPS
TERSE LASSIES EASIEST
```

Times One Only Once (page 167)

6	1	7	8	336
3	5	5	1	75
1	7	7	8	392
5	2	1	2	20
90	70	245	128	

Think ABCD Once More (page 167)

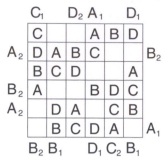

$$\begin{array}{c}
\; C_1 \quad\; D_2\; A_1 \quad\; D_1 \\
\end{array}$$

	C₁		D₂	A₁		D₁	
	C			A	B	D	
A₂	D	A	B	C			B₂
	B	C	D			A	
B₂	A			B	D	C	
A₂		D	A		C	B	
	B	C	D	A			A₁
		B₂	B₁	D₁	C₂	B₁	

(C₁ D₂ A₁ D₁ / A₂ ... B₂ / B₂ ... / A₂ ... / B₂ B₁ D₁ C₂ B₁)

Rhyme Time: Same Game (page 168)

1. same game; 2. yacht lot; 3. bet regret; 4. nice twice; 5. roast most; 6. hair repair; 7. grain train; 8. exude crude; 9. spring ring; 10. police piece; 11. swell barbell; 12. winner dinner; 13. mullet gullet; 14. receives leaves; 15. appliance alliance

INDEX